Wellington
Special

Alec Lumsden

LONDON

IAN ALLAN LTD

First published 1974

ISBN 0 7110 0527 3

Published by Ian Allan Ltd, Shepperton, Surrey
and printed in the United Kingdom by
Biddles Ltd, Guildford, Surrey

Author's Note

This book is the second of a new series which was begun with the *Spitfire Special* by Ted Hooton. To have had the opportunity of providing a companion volume on the Vickers-Armstrong's Wellington, the almost equally famous and contemporary aeroplane from the same Vickers stable as the immortal 'Spit' has been a great challenge. The Wellington was an aeroplane of great strategic importance and I have related this story to the times in which, and the troubles into which, it flew. Space does not permit more than a brief glance at some of the very important work of the Wellington. I have chosen therefore a collection of cameos and photographs illustrating how and why it came about (much of it new and extracted from the Manufacturer's own records) and something of its contribution to Allied victory. By no means is it intended to be the book to end all books on the subject. The vast amount of slogging work of this remarkable aeroplane and its crews requires a big book and, until such a full and definitive chronicle makes its appearance, it is my hope that this will provide an appetiser, an interesting and worthy tribute to an outstanding British achievement.

Acknowledgements

Writing a book can be a formidable task, especially so if it requires any serious research. Inevitably, it seems, every flat surface disappears beneath piles of papers and books. My wife is looking forward to seeing the dining table again as the piles of books are restored to their shelves. To her and all who have helped with photographs, with proof reading and advice, my thanks are offered. I hope that the result may prove as interesting as the other books which I have consulted and as accurate as the best of them. I should like to thank Messrs R. P. H. Yapp, a previous Managing Director of Vickers Limited, J. H. Robbie, CA, a recently retired Director of the Company, Sir Barnes Wallis and Hugh Scrope, the Secretary of Vickers Limited, for lending me much helpful documentation; Norman Barfield for photographs and much else besides, without which the book would have been a non-starter; and Arthur Sturgess whose admirable paintings decorate the colour pages. As for many other friends who have helped, perhaps I may list them alphabetically. They include:

Charles F. Andrews; Jack Beaumont; Norman W. Boorer; Charles E. Brown; Jack Bruce; Flt Lt Stanley Candy; David Dorrell; Eric Fielding; Flt Lt Alan M. Gardener; Charles Gardner; James Goulding; Robert C. Handasyde; Maurice Hare; T. H. J. Heffernan; Eric B. Morgan; John Motum; Philip J. R. Moyes; Arnold Naylor; Jim Oughton; Ken Smy; Flt Lt Alfred Price; the late Leslie Sansom; Jack Short; Theo Small; John W. R. Taylor; Ann Tilbury; Brian Wexham; Wendy Parkes, Ann Lifford and Christine Jennings who so patiently typed it all.

In addition, I specially want to thank Mrs Barrett, Reference Librarian, Ipswich Public Library for providing details of the crash of the B.9/32; Rick Barker, Librarian, The RAF Museum; Harry Cox, Reference Librarian, IPC Newspapers; and the very helpful staff of the Imperial War Museum Photographic Library and Air Historical Branch, Ministry of Defence.

Reference and Further Reading

I have also been greatly helped by referring to the following works whose Authors and Publishers I wish to thank. They are all recommended for further study:

Contents

Vickers, a History, J. D. Scott, Weidenfeld and Nicolson.
Vickers Aircraft since 1908, C. F. Andrews, Putnam.
The British Bomber since 1914, Peter Lewis, Putnam.
Armament of British Aircraft, 1909-1939, H. F. King, Putnam.
Squadron Histories since 1912, Peter Lewis, Putnam.
Aircraft of the Royal Air Force since 1918, Owen Thetford, Putnam.
Pictorial History of the RAF, John W. R. Taylor and Philip J. R. Moyes,
   Ian Allan.
Pictorial History of the Mediterranean Air War, Christopher F. Shores, Ian
   Allan.
Design and Development of Weapons, M. M. Postan, D. Hay, J. D. Scott,
   HMSO and Longmans.
Barnes Wallis, J. E. Morpurgo, Longman.
Aircraft Versus Submarine, Alfred Price, William Kimber.
Before the Storm, Robert Jackson, Arthur Barker.
Famous Bombers of the Second World War, William Green, Macdonald.
Bomber Squadrons of the RAF and their Aircraft, Philip Moyes,
   Macdonald.

I should like to express my thanks for being able to reproduce the
following:

   The words of 'Ops in a Wimpey,' taken from *Airman's Song Book,*
compiled by C. H. Ward-Jackson, by permission of the Publishers, William
Blackwood and Sons Ltd.
   The illustrations of Mr J. Wellington Wimpy in the 'Popeye' strip
cartoon, by permission of the *Daily Mirror* newspaper (IPC Copyright).
   Extracts from Training Memoranda are reproduced by permission of the
Controller of Her Majesty's Stationery Office. (Crown Copyright).

Front cover: One of Charles Brown's remarkable war-time series of colour pictures, this one taken in 1942 showing Wellington III, Z1572 of No 419 (Moose) Squadron RCAF, then based at Mildenhall, Suffolk.

Title page: A fine study of a Wellington II of 104 Squadron. One can almost hear the growl of the Merlin engines./*Charles Brown*

Above: No 38 Squadron changed from Fairey Hendons to Wellington Is in December, 1938. One of these Marham (Norfolk) based aircraft is seen at Northolt on May 23, 1939 when modern Service aircraft were shown to MPs and Air Ministry guests. The code letters NH were changed to HD at the outbreak of war./*Charles Brown*

Introduction

Many aeroplanes have captured people's imagination over the seventy years or so since the first powered flight by the Wrights. The Vickers-Armstrongs Wellington bomber is certainly one of them but today, some thirty years after its heyday in front line squadron service with home-based Royal Air Force Bomber Command, it is perhaps remembered more as a famous name rather than for any particularly spectacular exploit. Why this should be so is not easy to determine, for the Wellington had its fair share of excitement and glory in its day. Perhaps its very capability of tackling almost any job to which a large and capacious twin-engined aeroplane could be put was responsible to a large extent.

The Wellington, which started its Service life as a medium bomber in 1938, was the mainstay of Bomber Command (and sole equipment of the East Anglian No 3 Group) until late in 1940. By this time, the first ripples were to be seen, heralding the fast rising tide of big, four-engined bombers. The Stirling was the first and, weighing around twice as much as the Wellington, with a correspondingly greater bomb-carrying capability, these much larger aircraft—followed by the Halifax and Lancaster—started flowing in numbers to the squadrons from late 1940 onwards. At the same time, with the steadily increasing Allied bombing effort, more and more squadrons were being formed, particularly as the Empire Air Training Scheme got under way, providing the badly-needed crews.

Nevertheless, there was much for the Wellington to do, particularly after the invasion of the Low Countries in May, 1940. In fact, so much demand was there for the Wellington's services, and so adaptable had it become, that it began to appear in many other roles and in every other theatre of war, thereby proving its adaptability for tackling almost any work demanded of it. This included the dropping of 4,000lb bombs ('Cookies' or 'Blockbusters'); minelaying; minesweeping; submarine hunting; torpedo dropping; some of the earliest electronic countermeasures experiments; high altitude flying with a pressurised cabin; glider towing; troop and ambulance transport trials; and, inevitably crew training of all kinds. The Wellington was one of the greatest trainers of heavy bomber crews and continued in this work until its withdrawal from service in March, 1953—the last retiring from No 1 Air Navigation School at the end of that month.

Even then the geodetic construction—for which the Wellington had become so famous—continued to serve in its commercial successor, the Viking, in its initial form.

The very adaptability which made the Wellington so popular with the RAF accounted in no small measure for its being produced in greater numbers than any other multi-engined aeroplane built in Britain—11,461 all told. This massive figure needs to be considered in relation to the effort involved in the geodetic construction, for it was not at first sight the easiest or simplest to put together.

This is a story in itself (told in a later chapter)—the geodetic design devised by Barnes Wallis being possibly the feature people most associate with the Wellington, apart from its somewhat endearing sobriquet, the 'Wimpy'.

By common consent, the Vickers Wellington is among the top dozen most successful aircraft ever built and clearly justified the distinction of carrying the name of one of Britain's greatest soldiers.

The great re-armament programme of the 1930s with its 'shadow factories' and accelerated by the Munich crisis of September, 1938, spurred on the Wellington production run which lasted until after the War's end and resulted in its having a longer and more distinguished operational career than any other British bomber. When the Wellington went to war, it acquired an almost legendary reputation for withstanding battle damage, a capability which was largely due to the unique basket-weave geodetic construction—which itself has aptly and variously been described as a 'collection of holes linked together in the shape of an aeroplane', a 'knitted' or a 'cloth bomber'.

Not only did the Wellington form the striking force of No 3 Group; it became the backbone of Bomber Command in the critical early years of the War and went

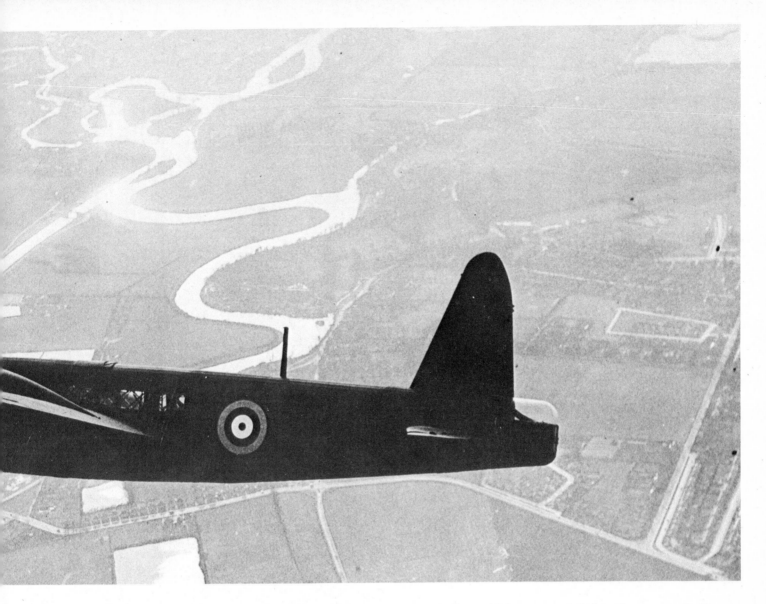

on to serve in all major theatres of the campaign with all RAF Commands (including Fighter), and eight Commonwealth and Allied air forces—still being front line equipment when the war ended in 1945.

Blooded in combat on the second day of the war (September 4, 1939), the Wellington carried the greater part of the bombing offensive on German naval and industrial targets for the next twelve months. Although it led the way in proving the value of the power-operated gun-turret, its first daylight operations were disastrous. These proved that even with this powerful defensive weapon, large bombers could not carry on the bombing offensive in daylight against heavily defended targets unless they had very strong fighter escorts. Unhappily for the Wellington in its early operations, the only high speed fighters in large-scale service were intended for short-range interception duties and quite unsuitable for such escorting. All British bombers had turrets mounting rifle-calibre .303in machine guns whose maximum effective range was about 600 yards. The opposing German fighters at the beginning of the war mounted 20mm cannon as well as lighter weapons and could attack in comparative safety from greater distances. At night however, the British guns in their multiple mountings

An early Wellington Mk I turns towards the late afternoon sun. For those with local interests, the old Walton Bridge lies beneath the Wellington's nose and Shepperton behind its rudder. Weybridge lies at the top left corner and the Wey is the left of the two rivers at the corner. Picture taken late 1938./*Vickers*

came into their own since fighting distances tended to be closer, particularly in the early part of the war prior to the wide-scale use of airborne radar by the Germans. The problem of daylight defence the United States Air Force was eventually able to overcome with its long range fighters and heavy .5in machine guns, when the next and more powerful stage was reached in the daylight war in the air. It was the Wellington and its gallant crews in the early stages of the war, however, which had revealed the true gravity of the problem.

Used to demonstrate the practicability of pressure cabins and the earliest jet engines and turbo-props at the end of its career, the Wellington provided the essential basic information on these two aspects of future airliner construction and operations which Vickers chose to pursue in strength when the war was over.

B.9/32-The Whys and Wherefores

To discover the origins of the B.9/32 specification from which the Wellington emerged, it is necessary to look back to the year 1909, the year in which Louis Blériot became the first man to fly the Channel in a heavier-than-air machine. As he landed at Dover, England effectively ceased to be an island. The air became a bridge which practically eliminated the protection of the stretch of water which British naval supremacy had guarded successfully for centuries.

All at once, Britain was vulnerable and indeed, just eight years later on June 13, 1917, London suffered its first raid by aeroplanes in the shape of fourteen multi-engined German Gotha G.IV bombers. There had been airship raids before this date but these vast, ghostly ships had seemed almost unreal, except for the unfortunates who were killed, injured or bereaved by their attacks.

The outcry demanding retaliation which followed the June raid of 1917 eventually resulted in the formation of the Independent Force, composed mostly of long-range bombers, under the command of Major-General Sir Hugh Trenchard. Previously Commander of the Royal Flying Corps, Trenchard was to become the 'father of the Royal Air Force'. His immediate objective was to build up the newly-created Independent Force and the ultimate target was Berlin. The biggest aeroplane then available was the massive twin-engined Handley Page 0/400, the answer to a demand from the Western Front for a 'bloody paralyser to stop the Hun in his tracks'. It could carry one 1,650lb bomb, one of the heaviest developed by the allies. It did not, however, have the range to reach Berlin with a worthwhile load.

There were, however, two new bombers under development for just this purpose, the twin-engined Vickers Vimy and an even bigger Handley Page V/1500. The first three of the 'Super Handleys', which had been delivered to No 166 Squadron at Bircham Newton (Norfolk), and which could reach Berlin from base, were ready to go three days before the Armistice was signed on November 11, 1918. The order to go was never given and Berlin was spared bombs for twenty-two years.

The end of the Great War found the newly fledged Royal Air Force with an inventory of 22,000 aircraft of all types, the most formidable air service in the world. This vast force was promptly run down on the grounds of economy, and an output of well over 3,000 aeroplanes a month flooding from the aircraft industry was reduced to a trickle—just enough to meet the needs of a Service which by 1920 had but 18 operational squadrons at home and abroad.

Britain's troubled Mandated Territories of Iraq, Palestine and Transjordan gave the RAF the chance to maintain its undoubted efficiency. The aircraft industry in consequence gained the experience required to develop long range bombing and transport aeroplanes. A result of this was the compromise bomber/transport, of which the Vickers Victoria and Valentia (developed from the capable but cumbersome Virginia bomber) were notable examples—following the Vimy, their distinguished predecessor which had made a name for itself with RAF bomber squadrons in the Middle East and as an Atlantic and Empire trailblazer. Vickers Aviation had thus become well versed in the long-range bombing and transport business.

The reconstruction of the RAF became an urgent necessity with the sudden realisation by the British Government that France had retained a combat force of 600 aircraft and was not showing any great friendliness to Britain. Mr Stanley Baldwin, the Prime Minister, stated in June, 1923 '. . . British air power must include a Home Defence Air Force of sufficient strength to protect us from an attack by the strongest air force within striking distance of this country'. A further 34 squadrons were authorised '. . . arranged with a view to the possibility of future expansion'. This provision was to be valuable later.

The start of it all. The Prototype Wellington B.9/32, K4049 in the classic Vickers setting, being wheeled over the River Wey from the Works to Brooklands aerodrome in May, 1936 some days before its first flight./*Vickers*

Three Wellington ICs of 37 Squadron. The nearest, LF-B is T2875, delivered at about the time the Squadron moved from Feltwell, Norfolk to Egypt where this Official Photograph was probably taken./*IWM*

Casting Their Shadows Before

In July, 1923, Trenchard (by now Chief of the Air Staff), called an Air Staff Conference. He remained as convinced as he had always been that attack is the best form of defence. He also propounded the principle that the bomber would always get through to its target unaided. Escorts had no place in his scheme and, in general, his Staff supported him. There were uncertainties concerning the differences between day and night bombers—would a single type be able to act satisfactorily as both a day and a night bomber? Should the day bomber be smaller, faster, more manoeuvrable? The night bomber could do without a lot of the protection needed by day and so carry a larger load. The CAS favoured the ability to carry a 4,000lb bomb if necessary. A member of the Air Staff, Squadron Leader Portal (later to become CAS himself) favoured the smaller day bomber although the development of separate types for day and night would cost more and slow overall production. The argument continued, but Trenchard's belief that the heavily defended day bomber would get through (and back) came to be tested with terrible results when war finally overtook Europe.

Despite the ominous build-up of air power abroad, particularly by Japan in the late twenties, the Cabinet continued to adhere to the 1919 'Ten-Year Rule' which assumed that no major war could be expected to break out for at least that period. In fact, in 1928 Winston Churchill, then Chancellor of the Exchequer, extended the Rule for a further five years.

At the Disarmament Conference in Geneva in 1932, Britain's case, *inter alia*, was that air bombing as an offensive weapon should be abolished. This commendable ideal made little progress however. Things were not made any easier when Germany walked out of the Conference and shortly afterwards announced its intention of building up an air force aiming at air superiority in Europe in defiance of the Versailles Treaty. The impracticability of the British disarmament proposal, and the difficulty of administering it if adopted, were highlighted by the outbreak of the first major war to occur since 1918 when the Japanese invaded China in 1932. Large numbers of aircraft were used and newsreel films of the war were widely distributed. This at least awakened the British Government to the possibility that war could spread from the Far East and to the realities of a re-emerging German air force much closer at hand. Indeed, in 1934, Mr Baldwin almost repeated his declaration made a decade earlier when he stated in the House of Commons 'This Government will see to it that in air strength and air power, this country shall no longer be in a position of any inferiority to any country within striking distance of our shores'.

Royal Air Force expansion was authorised to a first line strength of 128 squadrons. At the same time, Germany was announcing an expansion to well over half this strength by the following year. In 1935, following a visit to Berlin by the British Foreign Secretary, the Government initiated a vast expansion of the RAF, and none too soon. Italy was also on the war path in Ethiopia and the continuation of peace became more and more a forlorn hope. The Spanish Civil War in 1936 provided a bonus for Hitler and Mussolini for trying out their latest fighters and bombers against generally weak opposition—as did the Japanese in China. At this time too, was born the idea of the German-Italian-Japanese Axis.

The Cabinet's plans in the mid-30s included two particularly significant Schemes, 'C' and 'F'. Scheme 'C' called for 35 fighter squadrons and a bomber force of 68 squadrons to be available by March, 1937. One third of this force was to comprise aircraft which could reach the Ruhr industrial basin from British bases. A year later, in February 1936, Scheme 'F' superseded this plan which was already well underway. Scheme 'F' required the provision of twenty heavy bomber squadrons and forty-eight medium bomber squadrons based in the UK alone. Others were required overseas. A particular significance of this Scheme was its emphasis on reserves—75 per cent was to be available for immediate use, but a further 150 per cent should be available in reserve. A clear reflection of the bomber losses to be expected in war.

Wellington Is of 149 (East India) Squadron over Paris on July 14, 1939 (Bastille Day). The Squadron's code letters were changed to OJ soon afterwards./*Charles Brown*

An intimate shot of Mk IA, P9249 on test from Weybridge. The turrets are by Frazer-Nash./*Vickers*

The End of the Biplane

For several years before the expansion really got under way, the RAF bomber squadrons relied on interim aircraft, mostly biplanes and of somewhat doubtful value in the light of the large number of German monoplane fighters already known to be in production. The Fairey Hendon and Handley Page Harrow were the first of the (then) heavy bomber monoplanes. The Vickers Wellesley and Bristol Blenheim with their retractable undercarriages, flaps, and variable-pitch propellers, heralded the rapid elimination of the biplane as a medium and light bomber from 1936 onwards.

Since its creation in 1918, the Royal Air Force has never been without at least one Vickers aeroplane in first line service, and, indeed today, 56 years later, the largest and fastest passenger/freight transport in Strike Command is the Vickers-designed VC10. With the requirement in 1931 for a general purpose and torpedo bomber type to replace the Fairey III/Gordon/Seal, Blackburn Ripon/Baffin/Shark and Vickers Vildebeest/Vincent series, a specification (G.4/31) was issued by the Air Ministry for tender and most of the major manufacturers competed. The competition was won by Vickers which proposed two designs, a monoplane and a biplane. The biplane was evolved from the well proven Vildebeest design, via an unsuccessful prototype to the earlier (M.1/30) specification but introduced for the first time a novel, geodetic, form of construction in its fuselage devised by B. N. Wallis who had not long been working at Weybridge with R. K. Pierson, the Vickers chief designer. The monoplane's construction followed similar principles and was entirely geodetic. (The principles and construction of geodetic airframes are described in the next chapter.)

Against the wishes of Vickers, the biplane prototype was ordered but, at a board meeting on August 12, 1932, the company decided to build the monoplane as well, at its own expense. The eventual cost was £30,271. When both had been built, the monoplane, later to become the Wellesley, was far the superior in performance, a fact which caused Sir Robert McLean, Chairman of Vickers (Aviation) Limited, to write an impassioned letter to Air Vice-Marshal Sir Hugh Dowding (later Lord Dowding) in July 1935. He stressed to Dowding the desirability of building the monoplane rather than its biplane stable companion of which the Air Ministry had placed an order for 150 earlier that year. 'In my view,' wrote Sir Robert, 'it is not a modern machine.' He added that, until Dowding could decide whether the Company were to be allowed to build the monoplane, the Vickers Board did not wish to proceed with the biplane design. History records the result—orders for the Wellesley totalled 176 and the G.4/31 biplane was abandoned.

Seven months after deciding to proceed with the two contenders for the G.4/31, the Vickers board put forward a tender for the construction of a prototype all-metal twin-engined bomber in accordance with another Air Ministry specification—B.9/32. This required a range of 720 miles with a bomb load of 1,000lb—a modest enough demand. The design was of a high wing monoplane with a fixed undercarriage and either two 660hp Bristol Mercury VI or Rolls-Royce Goshawk I steam-cooled engines. A broadly similar design, the Handley Page Harrow, was put into production and so, later, was the Hampden from the same company initially also to the B.9/32 specification. In the light of further tests with geodetic construction, however, Vickers scrapped the original proposal under B.9/32 in October 1933 and made a start on a completely new design. This was to be entirely of geodetic construction and to have a mid-wing layout, two Goshawk engines (later changed to Bristol Pegasus), retractable landing gear and was in every respect technically advanced, benefiting from the Company's experience with the Wellesley.

Such were the merits of the light, basket-type of structure, combining high strength with light weight and permitting excellent aerodynamics, the new B.9/32 design from Weybridge would have a range of 2,800 miles with a bomb carrying capacity of 4,500lb—four times the requirement and slightly more than visualised by Trenchard ten years earlier. This new bomber was eventually to become the Wellington.

Above: On its first public appearance, the B.9/32 with its 'New Types' number 7 on the nose taking off at Hendon./*Vickers*

Left: The prototype of the long series of Wellingtons, K4049 built to Air Ministry specification B.9/32. The location is Weybridge, where it was built and based until its move to Martlesham Heath.

Below: Very early pictures of the B.9/32 in the flight shed and ground running its Bristol Pegasus engines./*Vickers*

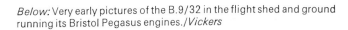

The Origin of Geodetics

Geodetic construction originated in the rigid airship as a result of the failure of the hull of Vickers dirigible 'Mayfly' in 1911. The airworthiness authorities then decreed that on no account would they allow gasbag mesh supporting wires to be attached to the longitudinal girders in the future. The reason was that, due to the difference in pressure between the top and bottom of the bags, and variations in the degree of inflation, uneven and largely unpredictable stresses could be imposed on these longitudinals. Now, if a loose wire is loaded equally along its length, it will form the arc of a circle. Unfortunately, a gasbag is not inflated evenly and its natural tendency is to take up an ellipsoid shape, rather than that of a sphere. So, to brace it satisfactorily with wires, it is necessary to devise a pattern of wires which will contain it equally throughout its surface. This would have been easy had the bags been attached to the longitudinals and had they been cylindrical—but they were neither. Various methods had been employed before but B. N. Wallis, who had been given the job of designing the structure of the R100 airship, had the idea of distributing the wire mesh so that the wires were closest together where the pressure was highest (at the top of the bags), gradually spreading out as they descended to the lower pressures at the bottom—the loading thereby being even all over the bags' surface.

Wallis sought guidance from the Professor of Mathematics at University College, London. After two weeks' calculations, the Professor told him that the lines he wanted were 'Geodesics'. From then onwards, Wallis' calculations were straightforward.

This was the origin of geodetic construction and followed the same basic principle employed by trans-Atlantic navigators—the great-circle, or shortest distance between two points on a curved surface.

Wallis applied his new ideas to aeroplane structures after he joined the staff of Vickers at Weybridge as a structures designer late in 1930 and proceded to develop a form of airframe structure based on geodetic principles. 'All I had to do' he said 'was to get from Rex Pierson the ordinates of the shape he wanted and then stretch a piece of string from point to point around its surface. I could cover it with geodesics'.

Wallis (later to become Sir Barnes Wallis) also believed that the high speed expected from modern aircraft could best be attained by the use of the monoplane with a carefully shaped low resistance form of wing and body. His investigations showed that the essential features of a successful monoplane should be: aspect ratio (span/chord) not less than nine or ten; a thickness/chord ratio at the root of the wing of not more than about 17 per cent. He argued that the weight of a wing of constant area and wing loading and designed for equal speed varies at a rather greater rate than the square of the aspect ratio when the thickness/chord ratio at the wing root is constant. Under such conditions, in stressed skin construction a wing of aspect ratio nine would weigh approximately three times the weight of a wing of aspect ratio six. This, he said, was the reason why most of the stressed-skin type monoplanes at that time did not exceed an aspect ratio of six or seven. Stressed-skin constructors had to choose between a relatively low factor of safety and its consequential low loading, or a very heavy structure. In Wallis' opinion, progress in the performance of aircraft was being blocked by these limitations. He had therefore set himself the task of getting out of that impasse by applying his airship experience to an entirely new system of aircraft structure which suited his theories perfectly.

Employing the aircraft's structural material in the dispersed or stressed-skin form, it was difficult to realise more than 40 to 50 per cent of the ultimate strength which the material could develop if it could be suitably supported. This deficiency could be overcome by the geodetic system which used the material in the most efficient form, i.e. thick concentrated section with a light fabric covering.

The result was a structure reminiscent of basket-work, the geodetic members being disposed diagonally in spiral fashion from end to end of the structure; a second

system—identical with the first in pitch, curvature, and thickness—girdling the structure in the opposite direction. The paths of the geodetic bracing members—which were ƍ-sectioned, about 2in deep and ⅝in wide—were so arranged on the surface of the streamline body that whatever combination of external forces was applied to the body, one system of geodetics was subjected to compression, and the other to tension loads. At every nodal point (i.e. points where the right and left handed systems of geodetic members intersected one another) the bars were firmly secured.

Wallis reasoned that when a curved bar is subjected to compression its curvature tends to increase, but this increase of curvature could be prevented by applying a series of lateral forces acting radially outwards and normal to the curve throughout its length. Similarly when a curved bar is subjected to tension its curvature tends to decrease, but this decrease can be prevented by applying a series of lateral forces acting radially outwards and normal to the curve throughout its length.

The paths of the curved geodetic bars were so arranged that at each node the centripetal and centrifugal forces required to maintain the compression and tension members respectively in equilibrium without change of curvature were exactly balanced; with the remarkable result that, in fact, practically all the effects of curvature

Left: The geodetic strips rolled and cut to correct curvature and length, are drilled, riveted into panels and bolted to longerons and frames at nodal points./*Vickers*

Above: The B.9/32 differed considerably in shape and construction from the production aircraft. The B.9/32 fuselage had top and bottom keel members and one longitudinal along each side./*Vickers*

13

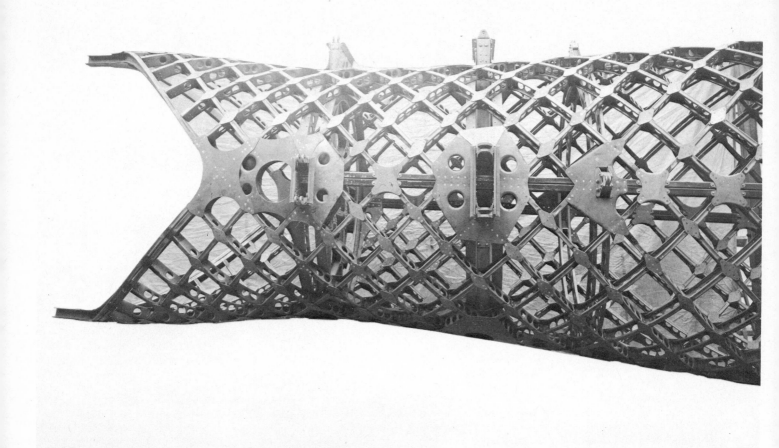

Noticeable differences between the rear fuselage of the B.9/32 and early Wellington./*Vickers*

are eliminated. Thus, the curvilinear or streamline shape was constructed without the addition of further fairings or falsework, requiring no more than a light fabric covering. The overall result was an extremely light and exceptionally strong structure with very high factors in both fuselage and wings (although, later, liable to fatigue).

When designing the wings of the Vickers Wellesley, advantage was taken of this reduction in weight to achieve an unusually high aspect ratio which was synonymous with high aerodynamic efficiency. Its performance proved that for a given power and comparable specification, it could carry heavier loads faster, farther and higher than machines embodying the usual type of construction. The world record for distance which the Wellesley won from Russia in November 1938 demonstrated this convincingly.

An idea of the weight/strength ratio of the geodetic system was given by the official report on tests carried out by the RAE on the fuselage of the Wellesley, when compared with an orthodox type of structure of identical specification requirements. These showed that the geodetic structure, although only two thirds of the weight, was more than twice as strong in flexure and nearly twice as stiff in torsion as the other type. The ultimate failure of the geodetic structure occurred at a factor of well over ten. It was as Wallis has said '. . . a self-supporting structure without any nonsense inside at all—nothing! A beautiful thing'.

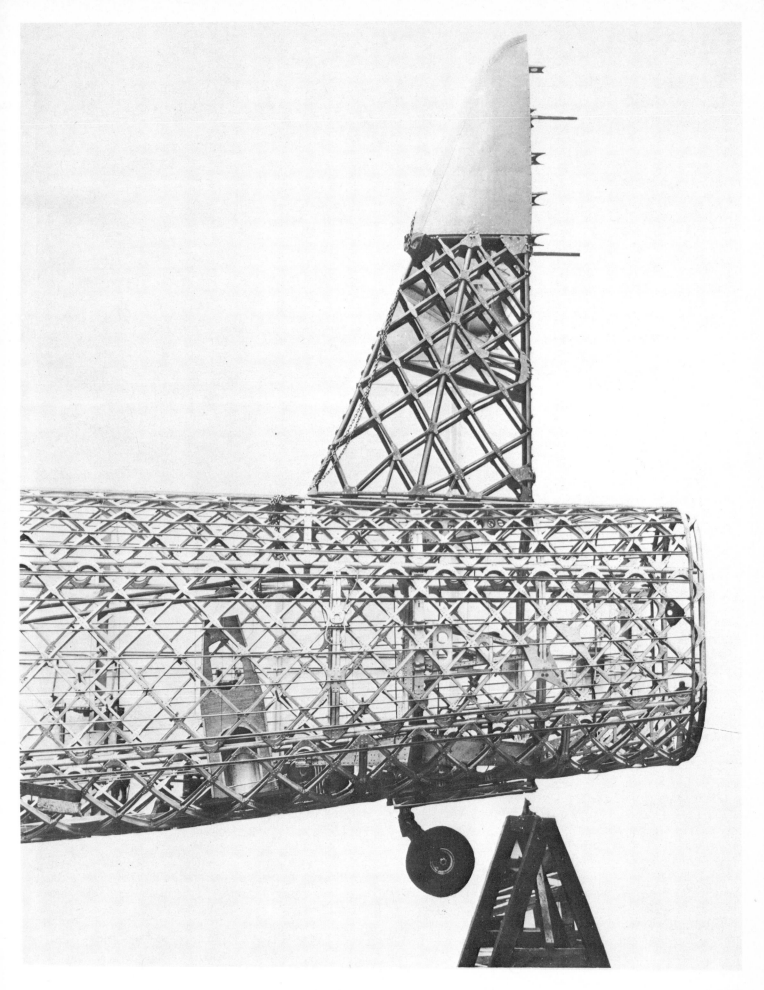

The Geodetic Family

It has often been supposed that the other large twin engined geodetic bomber of the World War II period, the Vickers Warwick, was built to succeed the Wellington but this is not so. The plain fact is that the Wellington and Warwick were both under construction while the Wellesley was in production. Vickers, like BAC which suceeded it at Weybridge, had seen the basic economics of having a family of related aeroplanes under development and construction. Perhaps the situation may be made clearer if the essential facts are stated in relation to each other. Specification B.9/32 which produced the Wellington called for a medium twin-engined day bomber. The Warwick, to a slightly later specification B.1/35 was, nominally, a heavy bomber. That is the relationship—though each aircraft had its own troubles which tended to obscure this. The B.9/32 was a very promising design and in 1935, some months before it flew, Rex Pierson, Vickers' Chief Designer, considered that, by increasing its length and span, the new requirements for a larger and more potent bomber could be met by using two of the new, much bigger engines then under development. A contract for a prototype to B.1/35 specification was issued on October 7, 1935 and construction began at once, about eight months before the B.9/32 flew. Naturally, the bigger aircraft had some refinements but basically the structure was similar. Owing to teething troubles with one new engine after another, the B.1/35 (Warwick) did not fly until August 1939. The B.9/32 however, went ahead well and made a satisfactory first flight from Vickers' aerodrome in the centre of the Brooklands motor racing track near Weybridge on June 15, 1936 in the hands of the company's famous Chief Test Pilot J. (Mutt) Summers. It was reported that, if a production order were received, the aeroplane would be named 'Crécy', although why and by whom this name was chosen has never been explained. A production order was duly received for 180 aircraft exactly two months after the first flight and the aircraft was named 'Wellington'. This order was for a redesigned version to Specification B.29/36 (Medium Night Bomber) and incorporated many detail improvements already designed for the B.1/35, notably powered gun turrets. The production aircraft was geometrically identical with B.1/35 with the omission of Stations 26-38 in the mid-fuselage, a smaller wing centre section, and identical outer wings.

Then came an unexpected setback. The B.9/32 crashed while nearing the end of its trials at the Aircraft and Armament Experimental Establishment (A&AEE) at Martlesham Heath, Suffolk. The cause was quickly determined—imbalance of the elevators at high speed. The redesigned Wellington now in production at Weybridge incorporated the lessons learnt from the crash and a revised fin, rudder and elevator design was developed from the B.1/35. Three gun turrets of Vickers design were installed in the nose, tail and mid-under positions, using Frazer-Nash controls, hydraulically operated.

Meanwhile, big brother B.1/35 (Warwick) languished somewhat while suitable engines were made available and it did not really get into its stride until 1943. The Warwick, whose final design slightly preceded the Wellington, and with which it was inextricably linked, never achieved the success it merited. Such success as it did achieve was in a different role. At that time, the Wellington was being phased out of front line service in home-based Bomber Command by the four-engined heavies which themselves had made a big twin like the Warwick obsolete through lack of performance. Nevertheless, the Warwick had pointed the way for the Wellington which in the end was built in far greater numbers than any other British multi-engined aeroplane before it or since. Including the B.9/32, a total of 11,461 Wellingtons was built at Weybridge, Chester and Blackpool. Deliveries altogether from these three factories averaged no less than 31⅓ Wellingtons per week throughout the production of seven years and two weeks. Peak production at one of the three main factories was of the order of 25 Wellingtons in a single week and, as a special effort, one was built in a single period of twenty-four hours.

The new shape in the sky, K4049 as it appeared in public for the first time in June, 1936 at the RAF Display at Hendon, soon after its first flight./Vickers

The sad end of the B.9/32. Elevator over-balance in a high-speed diving trial caused the aircraft to break up under sudden negative 'g'. The pilot, Flt Lt Maurice Hare told his flight test observer, AC/1 G. P. Smurthwaite to jump and undid his own straps. He found he could not move until, suddenly the aircraft pitched down beyond the vertical and began to break up. The pilot was thrown through the roof and slightly injured and his parachute appeared to open by itself. Smurthwaite struggled to reach a hatch but was unable to get out before the crash and he was killed. The picture shows the wreckage, inverted, near Waldringfield, 1½ miles east of Martlesham Heath where the B.9/32 had almost reached the end of its trials. The date was April 19, 1937./via Maurice Hare

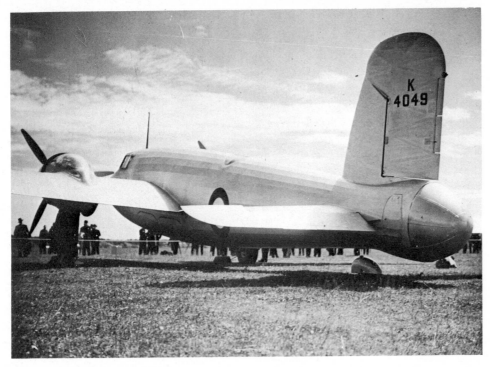

A revealing shot of the B.9/32 at Hendon. The geodetic construction of the aircraft was then still secret and nose and tail cupolas were covered to hide the interior from prying eyes. Clearly seen are the Supermarine Stranraer fin and rudder assembly and the exit for the rear gunner. The mid-upper turret position is also visible./Barratt's Photo Press

OPs in a Wimpy

The first production Wellington was delivered to No 9 Squadron at Mildenhall (Suffolk) in October, 1938 and, by the outbreak of war, six squadrons of Bomber Command were fully equipped and operational with MkIs. Four others were working up.

At 18 15hrs, on September 3, 1939, nine Wellingtons from Mildenhall (with 18 Hampdens from Scampton) took off on what should have been the first bombing raid of the war. They were briefed to attack German warships off the Danish coast but failed to locate them. Next day, fourteen Wellingtons (this time with 15 Blenheims) took part in the historic attack on ships of the German Navy at Brünsbuttel, and were badly mauled by German fighters. The following year, numerous sorties were flown as armed reconnaissances during the Norwegian Campaign and, after the German break-through in the Low Countries, Wellingtons attacked targets in support of the land forces. By this time, however, and as a direct result of the experiences in 1939, daylight operations within reach of enemy fighters were severely curtailed and finally had to be abandoned because of the Wellington's poor defensive armament. Later in the summer of 1940, Wellingtons on night operations bombed the German barges concentrated for the invasion of Britain.

Above: Wellington Is of 9 Squadron taking off from Evère Airport, Brussels, after visiting the Belgian capital for the Second International Salon of Aeronautics, July 8–23, 1939./ *Charles Brown*

Left: This shot of No 9 Squadron aircraft is an early one showing the twin aerial masts and the nearest aircraft with a D/F loop aerial. This also has the wind deflector screen on the sliding astro hatch in the open position. Later, plastic domes were fitted. Ahead of the windscreen is the outside air temperature thermometer and, beneath the nose, the venturi for driving the blind-flying instruments. The turret is one of Vickers design./*IWM*

Far left: A Wellington IC climbs away from Brooklands where it was built. The famous banked motor racing track lies in the background, camouflaged with bushes, and fat barrage balloons stand guard. The nearest to the runway has been hauled down while flying is in progress./*IWM*

OPs in a Wimpey

Of the many versions of OPs in a Wimpey, or Wimpy, this one (from 156 Squadron) was published in 'Airman's Song Book,' compiled by C. H. Ward-Jackson. It was sung to the tune 'Waltzing Matilda.' The less obvious initials are —CSC, Course and Speed Calculator and NFT, Night Flying Test. Holkham was a coastal gunnery range near Wells, Norfolk.

Who'll fly a Wimpey, who'll fly a Wimpey,
Who'll fly a Wimpey over Germany?
I, said the Pilot, I, said the Pilot,
I'll fly a Hercules Mark Three.

Chorus:
Who'll come a doing-ing, who'll come a doing-ing,
Who'll come a doing-ing, a doing-ing with me?
I'll come a doing-ing, I'll come a doing-ing,
I'll come a doing-ing in our Mark Three.

I'll pump the oil, Sir, I'll pump the oil, Sir,
I'll pump the oil, said the first W/op to me,
I'll take the rations out to the kite, Sir,
I'll get the rations from our Padree.

I'll set the course, Sir, I'll set the course, Sir,
I'll set the course on my little CSC
If you fly in on the course I set, Sir,
That will take us o'er *flak-ee.*

I'll shoot 'em down, Sir, I'll shoot 'em down, Sir,
I'll shoot 'em down if they don't shoot at me:
Then we'll go to Ops room and shoot a horrid line, Sir,
And then we'll all get the DFC.

I'll press the *tit,* Sir, I'll press the *tit, Sir,*
I'll press the *tit* at the first *flak* we see,
'Cos I don't like *flak,* Sir, I don't like *flak,* Sir,
Nothing but bags of height for me.

Let's do our air test, let's do our air test,
Let's go on up and do our NFT
Then we'll go to Holkham and shoot off fifty rounds, Sir,
(And save a few for HQ Group 3).

What about the Met, Sir, what about the Met, Sir,
What about the Met, it seems dud to me?
Let's scrub it out, Sir, let's scrub it out, Sir,
'Cos I've got a date with my popsee.

The First Blockbuster

As the early months of the war passed, Wellington production increased steadily. The aircraft itself underwent the normal process of development and improvement, such as the installation of the more powerful Merlin and Hercules engines and better armament. Wellingtons were now almost entirely employed on night bombing and, on April 1, 1941, a Wellington MkII delivered the first 4,000lb 'Blockbuster' to Hitler's Reich, on the port of Emden.

By May, 1941, there were twenty-one Wellington squadrons in Bomber Command, and a year later, of the 1,043 aircraft which took off to make the historic first of the three 'thousand bomber' mass attacks on Germany (Cologne) on the night of May 30/31, 1942, no fewer than 599 were Wellingtons. By this time, however, the four-engined 'heavies' were coming forward in increasing numbers and the Wellingtons were gradually phased out of Bomber Command, making their last bombing attack from England on October 8, 1943. They were still widely used by Coastal Command—Wellingtons were the first aircraft to use the Leigh-light for illuminating submarines and surface vessels by night after they had been picked up by radar. They were also used very widely for every imaginable training duty, both at home and in the Middle East.

Left: Parachuted sea mines were the stock-in-trade of the Wellington and very large numbers of these weapons were laid in enemy waters, the operation being code-named 'Gardening'./ *BOP, IWM*

Below left: The Type 423 modification enabled the Wellington to carry a 4,000 lb bomb ('Blockbuster' or 'Cookie') seen here being wheeled up to a Wellington III./*Charles Brown*

Below: A trolley load of 250 lb bombs about to be hand-winched into the bomb bay./*IWM*

Desert Air Force

It was, perhaps, in the Middle East theatre of war that the Wellington achieved its greatest fame, remaining as a front-line bomber until almost the end of the war. When Italy entered the war in 1940, the RAF had few suitable longe-range bombers in the Middle East but, late that summer, a small number of Wellingtons arrived from England. On September 19, 1940, aircraft of No 70 Squadron made their first night attack on the port of Benghazi. Attacks on this target continued almost nightly for many months and, 'The Mail Run' to Benghazi was immortalised in the 70 Squadron Song, to the tune of 'Clementine'. In Bomber Command, the Wellington had earlier been commemorated in the widely honoured RAF ballad 'Ops in a Wimpy'—sung to the tune of 'Waltzing Matilda'.

For the rest of 1940, throughout 1941, and for most of 1942, during the ebb and flow of the desert battles, the Wellingtons of No 205 Group attacked targets of various types. During the final advance of 1942-43, they moved to bases near Tripoli, remaining there until the end of the North African campaign. Wellingtons were also used by No 330 Wing of the British North African Air Force, operating from Tunisia.

In the summer of 1943, most of the Wellingtons were grouped near Kairouan, Tunisia operating extensively in support of the assaults on Sicily and Italy. During this phase, they made a number of remarkably successful attacks on railway bridges in Italy, using 4,000lb delayed-action bombs, dropped from a very low level. At the end of 1943, the Desert Air Force Wellingtons at last moved out of Africa to Foggia, Italy, and a wider selection of European targets came within their range. On April 8, 1944, for one special operation, they reverted to their 1939 role as day bombers, to attack with 4,000lb bombs concentrations of German troops in the Jugoslav town of Niksic. On the same day, they started intensive mining of the River Danube, the first of 18 such raids.

In the spring and summer of 1943, four-engined bombers became available for the Mediterranean area and Liberators started to replace the Wellington in 1944—but it was not until March 13, 1945 that their last operation took place. On that night, six Wellingtons accompanied a force of Liberators making an attack on the marshalling yards at Treviso, Northern Italy.

Right: Front turret (Frazer-Nash) servicing by a corporal of a squadron in 205 Group./*IWM*

Below: Five Wellington IIs of one of the squadrons in North Africa operated by 205 Group, RAF. Aircraft 'U' Z8624 has symbols of 52 operations on its nose and has had its front turret removed. Until the arrival in quantity of Hercules Mk Xs, the Mk II was used for strategic bombing against Axis military positions, supply columns and shipping./*IWM*

Above: An example of the blazing heat under which the crews worked in North Africa. Before a bombing raid on an Italian target, armourers prepare a Wellington X. The front gunner had, wisely, covered his turret and one can only guess at the pilot's remarks when he took his seat. His hatch is open. It was possible to fry an egg on a bare metal surface./IWM

Right: Wellingtons acted as trainers for paratroops. This Mk IC is loading trainees for their first jump at a Palestine base early in 1943—possibly 77 OTU at Qastina. The ventral turret position is used for dropping the parachutists, their exit being shielded by a lip just visible ahead of the tail wheel. This lip also helped to prevent the static lines fouling the tail of the aircraft./BOP, IWM

Wellingtons in India

The RAF's strategic bombing force in South East Asia included Wellingtons Mk IC, III and X. The Mk X illustrated is HZ950 of 99 Squadron and is waiting at a Burmese airfield as heavy monsoon rain approaches from the distant mountains. /IWM

The Japanese attack on the United States naval installations at Pearl Harbour, Hawaii on December 8, 1941 was made at about the same time as other Japanese forces landed in Malaya beginning the very rapid occupation of South East Asia. By mid-January, 1942, a new Group—No 225—had been formed in India to combat the Japanese threat and four months later the first Wellingtons arrived there. No 215 Squadron with MkICs made its first operational sortie on April 23, 1942. The Japanese at first had fighter superiority and most Wellington operations were carried out in support of ground forces under cover of darkness, often in difficult conditions of terrain and, in monsoon periods, extremely hazardous weather. As the home requirements of Bomber Command for Wellingtons became less pressing the first MkXs were released early in 1943 for reinforcing both Middle and Far East. The first MkXs to reach India re-equipped Nos 99 and 215 Squadrons and at once began the bombing of Japanese supply dumps from Indian bases. On November 16, 1943 the Air Command South East Asia was set up and systematic night attacks were intensified on Japanese occupied ports, road and rail communications in Burma and Siam, despite appalling weather which turned aerodromes into quagmires. Wellingtons continued to hammer the Japanese forces during the siege of Imphal, the turning point of the South East Asia campaign, and with their retreat in June, 1944, the handful of Wellington squadrons harried them by night in collaboration with fighter-bombers operating by day. By the end of 1944 the longer-range Liberators were becoming much more plentiful and superseded the Wellington as a strategic bomber, thereby releasing it for badly-needed transport work relieving isolated communities, troop transport and other less spectacular work but of the greatest importance in these inhospitable territories.

From Weakness to Strength

When the war began, there was no clear plan for the use of Bomber Command's rapidly expanding front line strength. Admittedly some aircraft were of a stop-gap nature. Some like the Fairey Battle which was deficient to a disastrous extent in defensive armament. Of Blenheims, however, there were substantial numbers. Both of these types were classed as day-bombers. The heaviest bombers in the Service were the Vickers Wellington and Armstrong Whitworth Whitley. These two aircraft, together with the Handley Page Hampden, were the mainstay of the Command. Initially, since the enemy did not at once attack the UK in strength, only limited attacks on the German Navy at sea and the dropping of propaganda leaflets over Germany were planned.

So began the 'Phoney War'—phoney, that is, to all but those who took part in it. The early raids were mostly by day against German Naval ships—navigation by night was not then a very exact science in the squadrons. The casualty rate among crew was shocking—particularly for the Wellingtons and one grave lesson, as we have seen, was quickly made clear: unescorted bombers by day were very easy prey to fighters operating close to base, particularly as the Germans already possessed an early form of radar warning. The RAF had no suitable long-range escorts. The bombers' defences were inadequate and, despite unbelievable gallantry in pressing home attacks on small and difficult targets, they took a severe hammering. The retractable under-turrets of the Wellingtons were almost useless, slowing the aircraft by as much as 15 knots just when they needed all the speed they could get. The turrets could not be used against high beam attacks and, in any case, the weight of defensive fire was minimal. The German fighters very soon worked this out and, almost at once, Wellington losses made two things imperative—to cease daylight armed-reconnaissance flights without fighter support and to provide better defensive firepower. This hastened the already planned introduction of Frazer-Nash turrets and led to the installation of window-mounted beam guns. The Wellington also had other serious weaknesses. It had no armour protection nor had it self-sealing fuel tanks. It caught fire easily and the fabric covering on the wings was soon destroyed. Those aircraft which did get home all too often did so with tanks drained through bullet holes or still gushing petrol. Lessons are quickly learned in war however, and modifications for installing armour plate and self-sealing fuel tanks were in hand within weeks of these early raids.

Despite these weaknesses, the Wellington was quite remarkably battleworthy and would still fly despite the removal of half its basket-like structure. Yards of its fabric could be torn or burnt off and on numerous occasions the Wellington still found its way home. Its susceptibility to fire remained its major weakness. (One man crawled out

onto a wing to put out a fire—and won the VC.) Its interior could be bitterly cold and was draughty at the best of times. Though its range was good, its speed (about 250mph) was unspectacular. Defensive armament was adequate at night and, had it had the mid-upper turret originally proposed for the B.9/32, it might have fared by day better than it did. Nevertheless, as a night bomber, despite its modest bomb-carrying capacity, it was very successful and highly regarded by its crews. Bombing was not its only operational role with Bomber Command and minelaying in enemy waters (*Gardening*) was a routine chore supplementing nightly attacks on communication centres, marshalling yards and other industrial targets.

Wellingtons were used at one time or another by at least 76 squadrons of the RAF and Allied air forces. They operated with Bomber, Coastal, Transport, Flying Training and Fighter Commands—the last for a brief time in one Flight of No 93 Squadron in 1941. Four Polish squadrons (Nos 300, 301, 304 and 305) and one Czech (No 311) operated the Wellington until it was replaced by Halifaxes and Lancasters. No less than 13 Canadian Wellington squadrons were formed, mostly in No 6 Group, Bomber Command. The first Commonwealth squadron, No 75 (NZ) was largely composed of New Zealanders, one of whom was Sgt James Ward, VC, the only winner of the award on a Wellington. Three Australian squadrons flew Wimpies (Nos 458, 460 and 466), and one South African (No 26) and one Free French (No 326) were Coastal anti-submarine units. Four RAF Wellington squadrons were named; No 99—Madras Presidency; No 149—East

A Wellington X with a nostalgic 'L-London' on its nose at one of the big group of bases at Foggia in southern Italy. /IWM

Before a raid, Mk IC OJ-N of 149 Squadron (one of at least five to bear this letter at some time) squats beneath trees at its dispersal point at Mildenhall, Suffolk in 1940. A refuelling bowser drawn by a tractor stands by its starboard wing, bomb trolleys with 250 lb bombs beneath the open doors. /Charles Brown

India; No 214—Federated Malay States; and No 218—Gold Coast.

In Bomber Command, Wellingtons served with Nos 1, 3, 4, 6 and 8 (Pathfinder) Groups and one squadron (No 69) with the 2nd Tactical Air Force (previously No 2 Group), used the aircraft on reconnaissance for a short time. No 8 (PFF) Group, a corps d'elite, operated Wellingtons in 156 and 109 Squadrons.

Coastal Command Wellington squadrons were, to a considerable extent, transferred from Bomber Command, although some were specially formed for general reconnaissance (GR) duties. Twenty-two Wellington squadrons in Britain, Iceland and the Middle East operated MksVIII, XI, XII, XIII and XIV Wellingtons at some time during the war, armed with torpedoes and depth-charges—reverting to or from bomber duties as the exigencies of war demanded.

Transport Command gained in strength and importance as the war progressed, requiring the conversion of bomber Wellingtons from quite early in the proceedings. These ranged from the CMkIs (later designated MkXVs) to the more rugged glider-towing MkXs. There were seven transport squadrons using Wellingtons at one time, although towards the end of the war every available bomber type was used as a transport for supply, rescue and troop repatriation purposes. In addition, they were operated by BOAC and, briefly, by No 29 Squadron, SAAF for transport duties.

No discussion of Wellington activities can omit the Operational Training Units (OTUs), mostly under Bomber Command. No complete list of units which used the Wellington has ever been published and it is doubtful if an authentic list is possible to compile, so ubiquitous was this versatile aeroplane. It was used for all sorts of jobs, from the specialist to the pilot training and humble target-towing for fighter OTUs. No doubt readers can add to the author's own list of Wellington units—which totals no less than 207. These are far too numerous to itemise but can be grouped under the following headings:

Air Armament School
Advanced Flying Schools
Beam Approach Training Flights
Central Gunnery School
Central Navigation School
Empire Central Flying School
Experimental and development units of various kinds
Ferry Training Units
Operational Training Units
Overseas Air Despatch and Preparation Units
Refresher Flying Units
Group Training Units
Target Towing Flights
Station and Communications Flights
Air Gunnery Schools
Air Navigation Schools
Armament Training and Gunnery Units
Conversion and other Training Units

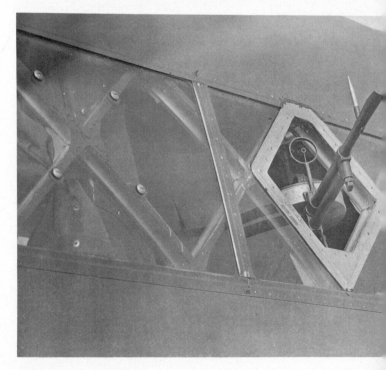

Left: Rear Turret (Frazer-Nash), two-gun unit showing entry doors which also give access to the fuselage. As shown it provides a parachute exit. Entry was an athletic performance./*Flight*

Below left: An early trial installation of a beam window-mounted Vickers 'K' gas operated machine gun in January, 1940./*Vickers*

Below: Major wartime bases of Nos 1, 3, 4 and 5 Groups in Bomber Command during World War II.

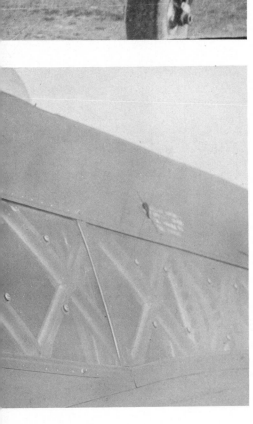

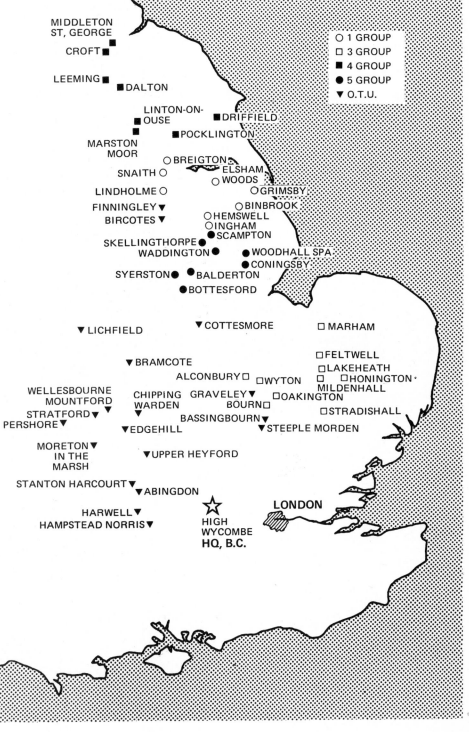

The Wellington's bomb bay was built as three narrow cells, each capable of holding six 250 lb bombs stacked in vertical pairs. The centre cell is shown./*Vickers*

Right: Wellington X, Chester-built LN710 releases a 500 lb bomb. It carries the markings of No 27 OTU, Lichfield, Staffs./*Aeroplane*

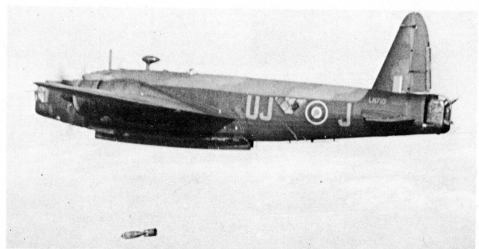

Below: The Wellington was successfully operated as a torpedo-bomber. The prototype installation was in Mk IC, AD646 which was tested at the Torpedo Development Unit, Gosport, early in 1942. The best dropping speed was around 100 kt at a height of 90 ft above the sea. After release at about a half mile from the target, to stabilise and arm the torpedo, the aircraft continued straight across the ship's bows. Curiously, this was the safest course./*IWM*

Sorties and Losses

Bomber Command alone suffered some 47,000 men killed in action and nearly 5,000 wounded—about 12 per cent of the UK's total Service and civilian casualties in World War II. These casualties were the result of 389,809 sorties on which 955,044 tons of bombs were dropped. The total losses of all types of aircraft was over 10,000. Wellingtons made 47,409 sorties with the Command (including 6,022 by OTUs) and dropped nearly 42,000 tons of bombs. In all, Bomber Command lost 1,332 Wellingtons on operations and a further 337 wrecked in accidents. On operations from the United Kingdom, Wellingtons flew 63,976 sorties totalling 346,440 hours flying. In the Middle East and Far East theatres of operations, flying hours totalled 524,769. Nearly 100,000 tons of bombs, etc., were dropped by Wellingtons. After the war, Wellington trainers flew a total of 355,660 hours. At an average speed of 150mph, the grand total of 1,226,869 flying hours represents over 184 million miles. In addition to this, wartime training probably exceeded another million hours.

A Blackpool-built Mk III, X3946 of 115 Squadron awaits a train of 1,000 lb bombs drawn by a tractor with a WAAF driver. This Mildenhall-based Wellington was lost on a mine-laying operation on October 16/17, 1942.

Above: Wimpies can take it. A badly burnt Mk III which demonstrates how the geodetic structure in the Wellington enabled it to absorb an incredible amount of battle damage./*IWM*

Left: A battered Mk IA undergoing overhaul by WAAFs at an RAF Maintenance Unit. At left is the rear turret of a Coastal Command Whitley./*BOP, IWM*

Right: Wing Commander John 'Moose' Fulton, DSO, DFC, AFC, surveys the result of a hit on one of the wooden blades of his port propeller. The aircraft is a Mk III and he managed to stop the propeller so that, in the wheels-up landing, no further shock loading would be sustained by the engine. The **Canadian 419 Squadron** which he commanded took its name from Fulton's nickname, following his failure to return from a raid on Hamburg on July 28/29, 1942./*BOP, IWM*

Night Fighter Attack

There were wide differences of philosophy between British and German bomber designers, at least in the early part of the re-armament race in the 1930s. British bombers were mostly equipped with gun turrets. Some of them were manually operated at first but later all were powered hydraulically, and these were mounted in bow and stern positions with upper and lower gun positions as well. The German practice tended to favour grouping crews close together in the forward part of the fuselage, somewhat cramped and with manually operated gun mountings. The German 'shoulder-to-shoulder' layout may have been good for morale but it had its limitations by comparison with the completely unobstructed fields of fire provided for British front and rear gunners, despite the isolation the latter involved.

The British policy paid off when cannon-equipped night fighters began to take their toll of the raiders attacking the industrial areas of Germany by night. The RAF were quick to learn how to combat these heavily-armed Luftwaffe night fighting Messerschmitt 110s and Ju88s. The method was simple but uncomfortable, at least for the rear gunners. The method devised was the 'corkscrew'—a climbing, rolling, diving, rolling and climbing manoeuvre. This was very difficult for the fighter to follow and usually forced all but the most tenacious to break off the engagement, wait until the bomber steadied on its course again and then re-engage using its radar. All of this took time and distance and, of course, the limited fuel the fighter carried.

On many occasions the corkscrew was successful and it called for the closest teamwork on the part of the bomber's crew. The pilot, because of his position and his need to rely on his instruments, could not watch his attacker who almost invariably approached at night from dead astern. From this position the night fighter crew could pick up and follow the bomber's engine exhaust flames. The bomber pilot was therefore very dependent upon his crew, particularly the rear gunner and whoever was manning the midships astrodome, for precise warning of the position and height of any attacker they spotted in the darkness.

The bomber's gunners were at a disadvantage in that the fighter's own exhaust flames were not easy to see from ahead. Once the fighter had been sighted and as far as possible identified, it was up to the gunner to tell his pilot what to do to make his evasive manoeuvres effective. At the same time the bomber's pilot had to hope that his instruments would see him out of trouble and that the artificial horizon would not topple. Fighters also worked very closely with searchlights which themselves operated in powerful groups. A bomber which was 'coned' by a group of lights was very hard put to it to shake off the lights and hence could be an easy victim of night fighters. The overwhelming brilliance of these lilac-hued lights, even to crews wearing dark glasses, made the reading of instruments a very difficult occupation indeed. The

bomber pilot therefore had to be both skilled in instrument flying and endowed with a highly disciplined crew if he was to find his target and survive.

The discipline required for this sort of exercise is well illustrated by the following contemporary story:

'I had the good fortune to be the rear gunner on an ideal Wellington bomber crew. Every man of the crew pulled his weight on the ground and, what was more important, in the air. . . . For each eventuality, each man knew exactly what was expected of him. Our normal procedure was for the 2nd pilot or the captain, when not at the controls, to be stationed at the astrohatch to give additional aid to the gunners in their plan of search for night fighters. This method had enabled us on several occasions to spot enemy fighters when some distance away; and by taking avoiding action immediately, we were always successful in losing them.

'On the night in question, there was a three-quarter moon and excellent visibility. We were returning from a sortie and did not expect any fighter opposition. We did not, however, relax our vigilance.

'About a quarter of an hour after leaving the target, following a successful attack, I spotted two dull red lights (or so they appeared) close together following us on the starboard quarter. These two lights were in the dark part of the sky, the moon being on the port quarter. There were no clouds nearby and no cloud to silhouette an aircraft against. Indeed, I was not at all sure at first that the lights were an aircraft; I warned the captain and immediately avoiding action was taken but the two red lights still followed us.

We then turned to starboard in a tight turn and went down in a dive. During this manoeuvre, I saw the silhouette of an Me 110* against the bright part of the sky and what I thought to be two red lights proved to be the

*War-time RAF terminology, later corrected to 'Bf110'.

34

A standard Mk II, W5442. This aircraft was one of four Mk IIs issued to 214 Squadron (W5442, 5452, Z8373 and 8490). These, together with five Mk ICs with Type 423 bomb gear, gave the Squadron its 4,000 lb 'Blockbuster' capability./*Vickers*

exhaust glow from his twin engines. We found that we could not shake the fighter off, so we turned back on course and our evasive action took the form of undulating. This fighter didn't appear to be a keen type and followed us, still on the starboard quarter, about our own height (11,000 feet) and at about 1,000 yards range. After five minutes had elapsed, the fighter closed in to about 800 yards, opening fire with two cannons. The range was, of course, too extreme for .303 Brownings so I held my fire hoping that the enemy aircraft would close and give me a chance to have a crack at him. But he was a very shy bird and when we throttled back hoping he would overtake us, he fell back too, and kept the range at about 800 yards. Every now and then, he would turn in and fire a short burst from his two cannons and then continue as before.

'This went on for about a quarter of an hour and having showers of explosive cannon bursting around the rear turret was far from comfortable. I was fully convinced that the only way to get rid of the fighter was to fox him into coming close to point blank range and shoot him down. I pause to remark that never for a moment did I doubt that I would get him first—why, I'm afraid I can't explain . . . that improved my morale 100 per cent. I asked the captain . . . when the fighter opened fire again, to dive down as though we were out of control and when I gave the word, to throttle back, lower the undercarriage and pull the nose up—everything to slow us down suddenly. The resulting dive was rather hair-raising and, of the whole encounter, was the only thing that really gave me the 'wind up'. The ASI registered 360mph in that effort which isn't bad for an old Wimpy. Jerry was completely foxed into thinking that he had got us and he came down after us, closing in to give what he thought would be the *coup de grâce*.

'What was most surprising to me, he came in from dead astern and when we throttled back, lowering the undercarriage, etc., we dropped from 360mph to 100mph in less time than it takes to tell. Jerry was taken completely by surprise and overshot. Instead of breaking away, he attempted to get his sights on us and when he found he couldn't get his sights to bear, he pulled up into a climb dead astern. The range during this was from 100 to 50 yards and I was firing longish bursts all the while.

'At this short range, I couldn't miss and I continued firing as he climbed away from us. When he got to about 500 feet above us, he stalled, turned over on his back and went down in a dive which rapidly became a spin. I last saw him 1,000 feet below, still going down. There was no indication that he was on fire or that the pilot had baled out. About 20 seconds later, there was an explosion on the 'deck' below us followed by a large fire which indicated that the Jerry had dug in. We then returned to base without further incident. I found on landing that in all I had fired about 300 rounds.

'Let me say now that most of the credit for this successful encounter goes to the captain, as he relied implicitly on my instructions without ever seeing the fighter and he did the right thing at the right time'.

Modest words, but a typical story of the sort of encounter the bomber crews faced nightly—no heroics, just cool professionalism. But what it does prove, if proof were ever necessary, is that power operated turrets in the hands of skilled gunners and in a strong, manageable aircraft like the Wellington, were very formidable defensive weapons. This one at any rate deserved its success.

James Ward -Wellington VC

Not all Wellington crews had it their own way, however. Although numerous decorations for gallantry and skill were won by Wellington crews, there is no doubt that many similar exploits unfortunately went unrecorded.

One which was, however, properly documented is recalled by the photographs on this page. Sergeant James Allen Ward won the only Victoria Cross awarded to a Wellington crew member. How he won it can only be a source of astonishment when the circumstances are considered. Ward, a New Zealander born in 1919, was a student teacher when, in July 1940, he enlisted in the Royal New Zealand Air Force. After training, he converted to Wellingtons at 20 OTU at Lossiemouth, Scotland and in June 1941 he joined No 75 (NZ) Squadron, one of the 3 Group Wellington squadrons based at Feltwell, Norfolk and which in 1940 had been transferred to the Royal New Zealand Air Force (RNZAF).

Sergeant Ward's seventh operation—on the night of July 7, 1941—was as second pilot of Wellington IC L7818. With 40 other 3 Group aircraft from East Anglian bases he took part in a raid on Munster in Westphalia, Northern Germany—just north of the great railway yards at Hamm which had been battered continually in attacks on the Rhur. Soon after setting course for return to base, the Wellington was attacked from below by a Messerschmitt 110 night fighter and was hit by cannon fire a bullet hitting the rear gunner in one foot. He delivered a burst of fire which sent the fighter on its way, smoking and it was not seen again. The Messerschmitt had, however, done its work and the crippled Wellington, bomb doors sagging open, and fuel leaking from a ruptured pipe in the starboard wing centre section, suddenly caught fire.

Quickly throttling back to as slow a speed as he dared, the Canadian pilot, Sqn Ldr R. P. Widdowson, ordered his crew to prepare to abandon the aircraft, but first to try to put the fire out, as it threatened to engulf the whole fabric-covered wing. Fire extinguisher and coffee flask were used to no avail. Sgt Ward had a look at the fire from the astro-dome amidships and then decided to try to climb out onto the wing and put out the fire with a canvas engine cover which was in use as a cushion. At first, he proposed to abandon his parachute to reduce wind resistance, but was persuaded otherwise. Despite protests by Sgt Lawton, a fellow New Zealander and navigator, Ward lowered the astrodome into the fuselage and, with a line taken from a dinghy tied to his waist, gingerly raised himself into the 90mph gale whipping past him along the top of the fuselage.

With the greatest of difficulty, Ward managed to kick holes into the smooth and taut fabric covering of the fuselage and was able to give himself enough hand and footholds to cling precariously to the outside of the Wellington. Fortunately, the wing was only about three feet below him—but it was burning in the same forced draught that was dragging at him. He managed to hang on, face down on the wing surface, gripping the structure with one hand and holding the engine cover in the other—somehow managing to persuade the flapping mass of canvas over the flames and into the hole in the fabric. Momentarily, the flames disappeared and for several seconds Ward held his arms in position. Then, as soon as he moved his hand, his arm by now being drained of strength, the cover was whipped away by the slipstream and the flames reappeared—but less intensely.

Unable to do more and near exhaustion, Sgt Ward crawled back the way he had come and, with help from the navigator, managed to regain the astro-hatch and comparative safety. As he recovered inside the Wellington, he saw the fire blaze up again briefly and then burn itself out. The captain set course for home and eventually a landing was made at Newmarket without brakes or flaps, the battered Wellington trundling to a stop against the boundary fence. It never flew again, the damage had been too great. But, due to the almost superhuman endurance of the young New Zealand co-pilot, it brought its crew home. Ward was awarded the VC and his captain the DFC. The rear gunner, who had scored a victory over the offending Messerschmitt despite his wound, was awarded the DFM.

Sadly, two months after this flight, Sergeant Ward's aircraft, of which he had been made captain, was hit by flak while on a bombing raid over Hamburg. Wellington IC X3205 fell in flames and only two of the crew escaped. James Ward was not one of them and he was later buried in Ohlsdorf Cemetery, Hamburg. His memory has been perpetuated, however, in one of the Galleries (No 6) at the Royal Air Force Museum at Hendon which is dedicated to winners of the Victoria Cross and George Cross.

How a Victoria Cross was won. Sergeant
J. A. Ward, RNZAF (No 75NZ Squadron) put
out a fire (A) caused by flak in this Mk IC
L7818 of which he was co-pilot when it was
returning from a raid on Munster on July 7, 1941.
He climbed out of the astro hatch (B), kicked
holes in the fabric (1, 2 & 3) and stuffed an
engine cover in the hole in the burning wing./
IWM

Ditchings

Crossing the water in wartime could be a dangerous business and an elaborate air/sea rescue service was organised because battle damage and shortage of fuel provided the hungry seas round Britain's coasts with plenty of aircraft and their crews. The Wellington was unusual in being provided with floatation gear as well as the usual dinghy. Flotation equipment was not itself new. Fleet Air Arm aircraft had been equipped with it in various forms for years, operating as they did from aircraft carriers.

The Wellington boasted 14 inflatable flotation bags stowed at the top of the bomb cells. Inflation was from three CO_2 cylinders which were stowed in the inner wings. These were operated by levers mounted on the rear of the centre-section spar. An immersion switch, mounted immediately aft of the front turret, automatically inflated the bags on contact with salt water. The drill before ditching was to ensure that bombs, depth charges, mines, etc, were dumped and then to close bomb doors and inflate the bags at least five minutes before ditching to ensure full inflation (and not above 3,000 feet). This gave the doors the appropriate support and without this, they would collapse and the chances of the bags inflating was remote. Torpedo-dropping Wellingtons could not carry flotation gear.

There were windows at the rear end of the bomb bay through which the crew could check that the bags were inflated. All of this had to be done and checked very quickly, more often than not in complete darkness by means of a torch, usually at low level and in bad visibility, perhaps with one engine dead or even on fire, and all too often with both engines dead for lack of fuel. A ditching in such circumstances was hazardous in the extreme and crew training and discipline were of the utmost importance.

An analysis made in 1942 of a number of Wellington ditchings showed that anything from 30 seconds up to ten minutes—but more often 1-3 minutes—might be expected before the aircraft went under. If the floatation gear was operated this allowed the maximum time but, in any case, this was all too brief especially if there were injuries among the crew and obstacles in the way of the escape exits. In 24 ditchings which were analysed, there were 124 crew members and, of these, 6 were killed, 17 missing, 6 injured, 12 slightly injured and 101 unhurt. In several cases, the crews were caught unawares by the impact while moving about inside their aircraft while, in others, crews simply did not bother to take up good ditching stations. These emphasised the importance of drill and knowing what to do automatically. Crew members were expected to be seated, braced with their backs against the rear step in the cabin or, in the case of the rear gunner, remaining in his turret so as to help the pilot by counteracting increasing nose-heaviness at the stall. Pilots were supposed to keep their Sutton harness tight and the

upward-operating hatches above their heads closed until the last minute, to reduce drag. The astro-hatch had to be removed inwards before ditching. All safety precautions had to be taken before touching the sea because of the risk of injuries and subsequent incapacities caused by sudden deceleration and damage.

Since landplanes were not designed for alighting in the sea, warned an official pamphlet, it was important to make the approach as near as possible to horizontal and at the lowest safe speed. The average approach speed estimated from 16 ditchings was 74mph IAS. Flaps should be lowered 30 degrees (not more to prevent digging in). At night, the landing lamp could be a help. In every case investigated, the dinghy inflated properly, although it could become inverted and entangled in cordage. The dinghy ('J' type) was stowed in the starboard engine nacelle, in the hump behind the fireproof bulkhead, and inflated automatically when the immersion switch was flooded. If this failed, there were manual releases in the fuselage and under a fabric patch on the starboard wing centre section. The dinghy carried emergency survival packs although some aircraft carried these separately inside the fuselage.

The official investigation came to the conclusion that casualties from ditching Wellingtons were surprisingly low but would be lower if crews learned their drill. Training in 'ditching' was steadily improved and the Wellington experience served Bomber Command crews well throughout the war.

A mine-laying casualty. Wellington III, Z1615 of 9 Squadron operating from Honington, Suffolk was presumed hit by a flak ship while mining the Great Belt, Denmark on May 16, 1942. Despite the aircraft's broken back, all but one of the crew (Sgt A. Gruchy, WOP/AG) survived to be taken prisoner. The tailplane stands vertically./*J. Helme*

A misfortune for the crew of Mk IA, P9218 of 149 Squadron (OJ-O). The aircraft was hit by light flak over Aalborg, Denmark on April 21, 1940 and the crew was taken prisoner./ *J. Helme*

Inflatable flotation bags were a feature of the Wellington. These were mounted in the bomb cells, shown stowed and inflated./*Vickers*

Wellington Production

The B.9/32, like its predecessors from the Vickers design team, was built at Weybridge. The factory was one of two major works alongside the kidney-shaped Brooklands motor racing track, the other being that of Hawker Aircraft Ltd which was to assemble Hurricane fighters in large numbers. The Government foresaw the need for dispersal, should there be a war, and so set up the remarkable 'shadow factory' scheme following the decision in the mid-30s to inaugurate a major expansion programme. Several large factories were established in the Midlands and North of England for the production of aircraft and engines, away from the well-established aircraft works whose locations, being mainly in the South, were known to the enemy. Nearly all shadow factories were managed by the motor industry. The Wellington was not, in the event, built under the motor industry scheme, although the idea had been considered to an advanced planning stage, at the big Nuffield works at Castle Bromwich, Birmingham, but Spitfires were built there instead. Vickers had planned a dispersal factory of its own at Hawarden near Chester, sharing the aerodrome with the RAF. A second plant was later built at Squires Gate on the outskirts of Blackpool. The Hawarden factory flew its first locally assembled Wellington on August 2, 1939 while the first Blackpool aircraft came off the line the following year. These two works between them built nearly four times the number built by the parent factory at Weybridge but they were purpose-built and laid out more spaciously for high rates of production.

When the first order for 180 Wellingtons was received at Weybridge on August 15, 1936, the manufacturing space and numbers of personnel were immediately increased. At the end of the year, T. C. L. Westbrook transferred to Weybridge as Works Manager from the Supermarine factory at Southampton where he had held the same position. Prior to the setting up of the Chester factory, a sub-contract had been placed with the Gloster Aircraft Company for 100 MkI Wellingtons. These were to be followed by a second batch of 100 of the projected Merlin-engined MkII. Later, another order which had been placed with Sir W. G. Armstrong Whitworth Aircraft Ltd at Coventry for 64 aircraft was transferred to the new Blackpool factory and the Gloster contracts were likewise withdrawn and transferred to the new Chester works. Weybridge began to get into its stride building Wellingtons and the first one to near-production standard was flown two days before Christmas, 1937. As production built up in the years 1938-39, enormous strides were made in the aircraft industry's output and Vickers-Armstrongs were no exception. The design team led by R. K. Pierson and supported by T. C. L. Westbrook and G. R. Edwards in Production and Experimental departments made the Wellington a manageable product and the production difficulties, despite the fiddly complexity of the geodesics, were overcome to the extent that only a handful of key Weybridge people had to be transferred to each of the northern factories. The remainder, most of whom had never worked in a factory, were recruited locally.

Few, if any military aircraft can have achieved so much for so modest a financial outlay as the Vickers Wellington. The initial order for 180 airframes was for the incredible figure (by today's standards) of £10,000 each.

So great was the Wellington production rate that the jigs were eventually written down to a mere £250 per aircraft. So involved was the sub-contracting effort that, for a time, there was no means of stopping production—even if this had been desired. For its complexity, its Meccano-like construction which demanded total allegiance to the god 'Jig', the Wellington was put together remarkably quickly. It is not without significance at Chester, for instance, that 68 per cent of the final assembly workers were women. The gentle art of fabric covering, for many years regarded as the job for which they were ideally suited (complicated in the Wellington by the need for wire reinforcement) was by no means their only contribution. At the peak of production, no less a personage than the Head Foreman of Final Assembly was a young woman.

The Chester works (Broughton—named after a nearby village) was conceived in September, 1936 as a Vickers-Armstrongs factory and was changed to a Government-owned, Vickers-managed shadow factory in 1938 for the sole purpose of building Wellingtons. The essential peculiarity of Chester was that it was planned as a mass-production assembly plant, not as a manufacturing unit. The whole plant was laid out and built on the concept that components would come in to be assembled. This was quite different from Weybridge where aircraft were built from raw material to finished aeroplane. So, too, was the Blackpool factory which, in many respects, was simply a duplication of Weybridge.

Components fed into Chester were provided by some 500 sub-contractors. As designed, the works had no machine shops other than millwrights shops. This was an important peculiarity of Chester at the beginning, although the factory did not continue that way. There were no parts stores in the initial factory design, components being fed straight on to the production line. Nothing was held in stock and, each day, so many components would arrive in order to build so many aeroplanes. This could not last and, as the tempo increased, large stores were built up. Chester was a remarkable factory in other ways. It was based on a huge assembly shop, some 400 yards long, at the end of which was an unsupported roof area of 650 feet square—in its day, the largest such span in Europe. It was completely traversed by a crane which could lift at any point up to 10 tons using two 5 ton cranes. Complete wings could therefore be lifted over the fuselage line for assembly in minutes. Twenty years later, when de Havilland were building Comets in the factory, they were able to do the

same thing in hours which would otherwise have been days.

The Blackpool factory had an unlucky start. A serious accident occurred on August 9, 1940 when, after the major part of the main works construction had been completed, the centre section of the main aircraft erection bay suddenly collapsed, killing six men and injuring twelve. Considerable delay in production ensued.

Sub-contracting was undertaken by an enormous variety of firms in support of Weybridge, Chester and Blackpool; almost any company, however small, which could turn its hands to metal-working of any kind was brought in. One of the obvious peculiarities of the Wellington and its geodetic construction was the enormous number of small parts. These were of almost infinite variety in their lengths and radii of curvature. One of the first things which had to be devised at Weybridge before even the Wellesley could be put into production was a clever but ingenious rolling mill which, by the simple expedient of altering the location of cams, enabled the lipped channel sections of varying curvature to be produced easily and quickly from light-alloy strip. When a geodetic panel was to be assembled, the worker concerned was issued with all the necessary parts, all of which had been checked for length and curvature, exactly as a Meccano toy might be assembled—the analogy is

The Weybridge works of Vickers Armstrongs in 1943. Two Warwicks can be seen. St George's Hill Golf Course is in the background./*Vickers*

inescapable. In the Midlands, three firms undertook all the rolling mill work for the geodetic construction at Chester. This was the only way in which it could have been made economical and only high production rates could justify tooling up by sub-contractors.

The Blackpool factory was started from Weybridge, not from Chester as might be supposed. The factory had its own sub-contractors and was much bigger than its near-neighbour and had its own machine shops from the outset. Weybridge was so vulnerable to enemy air attack that a complete duplicate unit was considered advisable.

The first Chester contract from the Air Ministry in May 1939 (prior to the formation of the Ministry of Aircraft Production) was for 750 Wellington airframes. Chester turned out 3 MkIs, following by 17 MkIAs and then settled down to turn out 1,583 MkICs. The first Chester-built Wellington I (L7770) was assembled, largely from Weybridge parts, in a Bellman-type hangar (the main works was not ready) and so bad was the drainage and subsequent flooding of the aerodrome at that time that it had to be flown to Weybridge for testing.

Weybridge, in addition to its general Wellington production (2,514 in all), did trial installations, modifications, etc. and produced such special Marks as the pressure-cabin MksV and VI. The shadow factories concentrated on the hard, slogging mass-production.

Blackpool's first contract was for 500 Wellingtons and the first three of these were delivered on September 30, 1940. Only 50 Pegasus-engined MkICs were turned out at Blackpool but no less than 2,534 powered by Hercules engines. These included 1,369 MkXs. Chester's output, more than half as many again, was 5,540 Wellingtons including 2,434 MkXs. This Mark, the best of them all, was also the most numerous.

Geared from the outset for high production, the Chester factory staged an exercise in which a complete aircraft was assembled from parts in one day. This exercise, by way of being a morale booster, was photographed stage-by-stage by the Crown Film Unit, and the aircraft—'Broughton Wellington'—got away with barely 30 minutes to spare!

Output from each of the northern factories reached 15-20 a week although these figures were greatly increased at times following bad weather periods and delays in component supplies. The numbers of aircraft flight-tested by individual pilots (and there were very few of them at each works) was remarkable. Maurice Hare, who was transferred from Weybridge to Chester as chief test pilot flew just over 3,000 aircraft on test. Besides Wellingtons,

these included 260 Avro Lancasters and 11 Lincolns which Vickers built when Wellingtons were finally phased out at Chester. Vickers test pilot Tommy Lucke once flight-tested twelve Wellingtons in a single week-end.

Weybridge was the only Wellington factory to suffer bomb damage. As had been feared, it was an easy target. Heavy bombing of aircraft factories by the Luftwaffe was part of its tactics in the Battle of Britain. At Weybridge, Hawkers was an obvious target with its Hurricane assembly line. On September 4, 1940, 14 Messerschmitt Bf110-C4s, half of them fighter-bombers and the others escorts, made a low level attack in which, unfortunately for Vickers, six bombs struck the main Wellington assembly hall. * Hurricanes from 253 Squadron at Kenley quickly disposed of six of them but not before 84 people had been killed in the works and another 300 injured. Fortunately, it had been the lunch hour or the casualties would have been far worse. Lord Beaverbrook, Minister of Aircraft Production, visited the works a few hours later and gave orders for manufacture to be dispersed forthwith with only final assembly to take place at Brooklands. It was nearly eight months before output was back to the pre-raid figure.

Sub-contracting on a very wide scale followed and, at one time, Weybridge had 536 dispersal units. These ranged from garages doing machining to a dance hall housing tubes and fabric stores; from film studios making wings to two out-buildings at the home of a lady in Station Road, Chertsey used as stores for finished parts. Carter Paterson (later to become part of British Road Services of today) had a machine shop; the Amalgamated Dental Co Ltd became fitters; Burhill Golf Club House became a

*c.f. *Battle of Britain*, Francis K. Mason, McWhirter Twins, pp 348-350.

design office; and bomb beams were made at Dartnell Park Gymnasium, West Byfleet. The complete list is too long to reproduce but almost every square foot of usable covered space in the local area seems to have been taken over. Numerous dispersal depots for stores, as well as component assembly, were also established by Chester and Blackpool. Each also had its secondary assembly line—Weybridge at Windsor Great Park (Smith's Lawn), Chester had Cranage and Blackpool had Stanley Park.

In all, 11,460 production Wellingtons were built. The basic shape was unaltered from start to finish. Four types of engines were fitted—Bristol Pegasus and Hercules, Rolls-Royce Merlin and American Pratt and Whitney Twin Wasp. Apart from a continuous 'beefing up' of the structure to take the ever-increasing gross weight, improvements in materials, armament, etc., the basic structural concept proposed by Barnes Wallis was amply vindicated. The aerodynamics of the Wellington were such as to require very little alteration to its shape, apart from relatively minor changes to the tailplane on the MkII

As recorded elsewhere, the Wellington was generally a pleasant and forgiving aeroplane to fly. It suffered a marked nose-up trim when flaps were lowered but this was partially eliminated by linking the flaps to the elevator trim tabs. The very flat angle of the fuselage when on the ground resulted in quite a number of broken tail wheels when it first came into service because of pilots unfamiliar with the aircraft attempting to hold off prior to landing with the stick too far back. The very flexible nature of the wings caused misgivings to some crews unaccustomed to this and curious manifestations sometimes occurred in the fore and aft movements of the control column—due no doubt to a 'lazy tongs' effect in the fuselage structure.

A Wellington's fuselage frames (not in correct sequence)./*Vickers*

Fuselage assembly comprises transverse frames, side, top and bottom geodetic panels, interconnected by four tubular longerons./*Vickers*

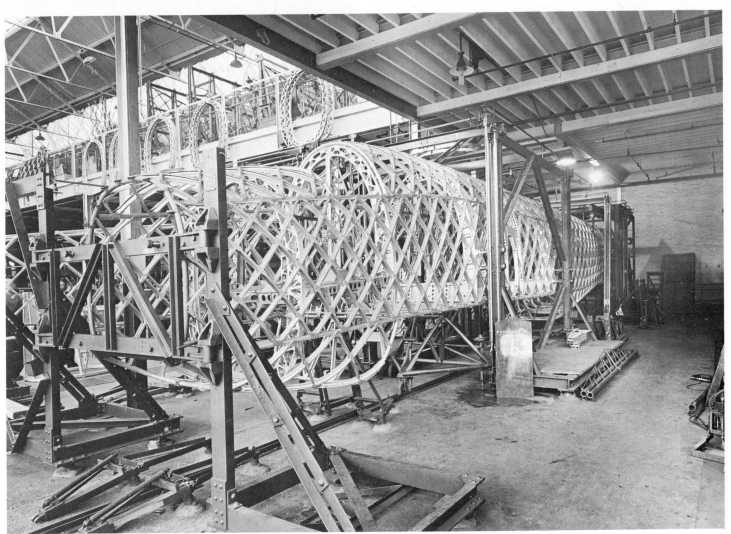

Left: The main spar floats freely through the fuselage, connecting loads between wings and fuselage being transferred by front and rear spars via a heavy root rib which is bolted to the main fuselage frames. This is the front spar attachment./*Vickers*

Below: A train of fuel tanks ready for insertion in the unobstructed wing of an early Wellington I. Soon after war began, self-sealing covering was fitted to reduce the risk of fire and fuel loss./*Vickers*

Right: A wing repair shop in 1941./*Central Press*

Below right: Women were expert fabric workers, seen here covering a geodetic panel./*Vickers*

The erecting shop at Blackpool in 1944, with Mk Xs, left, and XIVs at right./*Vickers*

Colour Plates

A. The B.9/32 Wellington prototype.

B. Wellington Mk IC, HX682 converted to DWI Mk II (Directional Wireless Installation) at a Middle East RAF Maintenance Unit in 1942 using degaussing ring components supplied from Vickers. It was operated by 162 Squadron based in Egypt.

C. One of thirteen Canadian squadrons which operated Wellingtons, No 425 (Alouette) Squadron, RCAF used the code letters KW. This Mk III, X3763 was built as one of the first production order at Blackpool. It failed to return from a raid on Stuttgart on April 14/15, 1942.

D. A General Arrangement drawing depicting Wellington X, LN710 in the markings of No 27 OTU at Lichfield, Staffordshire. The aircraft was built at Chester.

E. A typical Mk VIII of Coastal Command. The white side and under surfaces were proposed in 1941 by Professor E. J. Williams, a scientist from Farnborough who joined an operational research section at Coastal Command under Air Marshal Bowhill (later Sir Frederick Bowhill), the C in C. Previously, Coastal aircraft had been painted the same as those of Bomber Command.

F. High-altitude Wellington prototype Mk V, R3298, powered by GEC turbo-supercharged Bristol Hercules XI engines in 1940. These early experimental superchargers were not used on production aircraft and Merlin Series 60 engines were substituted while on the line.

G. Z8570, the first Wellington to have a tail-mounted Whittle-type jet engine, the W2B. It was a modified Mk II with Merlin X engines. (Type 445.)

A

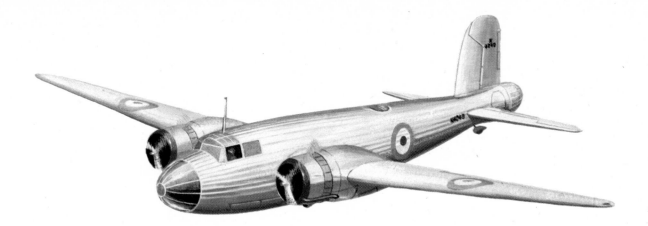

B

C

0   5   10   15   20
FEET

E

F

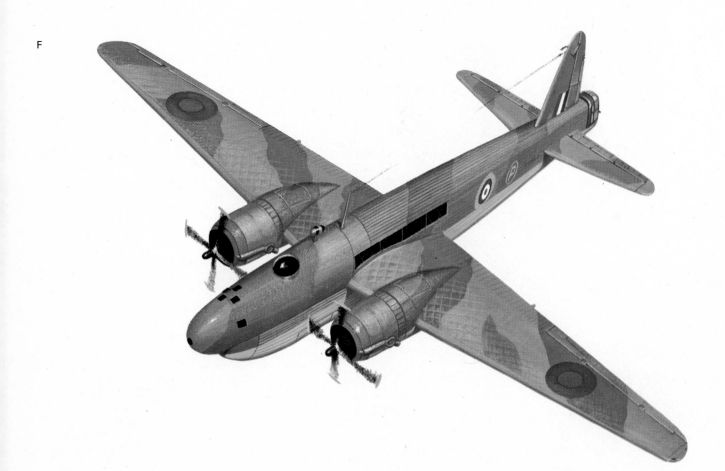

G

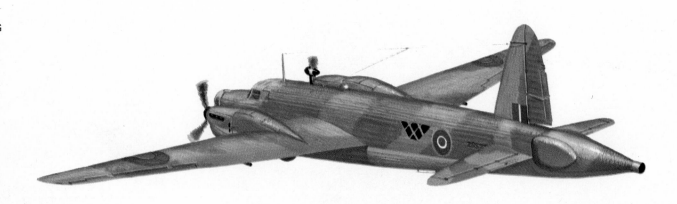

People

Two people who were intimately concerned with the development of the Wellington discuss its civil successor, the Viking. Left, G. R. Edwards, chief designer (now Sir George Edwards, OM, FRS, Chairman of British Aircraft Corporation) and the chief test pilot of Vickers-Armstrongs, J. 'Mutt' Summers./ *Vickers*

The man who was appointed chief designer of Vickers in 1914 and who held this position until he was appointed chief engineer in 1945, R. K. Pierson. He was responsible for all Vickers designs during this period including the Wellington./*Vickers*

Left: Inventor extraordinary and father of geodetic construction, Sir Barnes Wallis, CBE, a recent picture./*Vickers*

Far right: R. C. Handasyde, test pilot and former flight test observer./*BAC*

Men of Chester.
Right: B. A. Duncan, general manager, Chester./*Vickers.*
Above right: R. P. H. Yapp, commercial manager (later managing director, Vickers Ltd)./ *Vickers.*
Far right: Maurice Hare, chief test pilot, Chester./*Vickers.*

Know Your Wellington

Type
Twin engined medium bomber.

Wings
Mid-wing, cantilever monoplane; aspect ratio 8.83 light alloy Vickers-Wallis construction on geodetic principles. Wing built in inner and outer sections connected through engine nacelles. Inner wing attached to fuselage by reinforced inner ribs, the single Warren truss main spar (pin-jointed at centre line) passing through, but not attached to, fuselage. Auxiliary spars fore and aft attached to inner ribs and fuselage main frames. The rear spar carries split flaps and Frise ailerons. Wing panels fabric covered before assembly.

Fuselage
Four tubular longerons act as pickup points for nodal points of intersecting geodetic members. Fuselage fabric covered, oval sectioned and jig-assembled on two fabricated main frames at wing attachment points. Other principal frames at tail attachment and cockpit wall. Bomb-bay divided longitudinally into three cells. Later Type 423 accommodated 4,000lb bomb.

Tail unit
Cantilever monoplane, geodetic construction, fabric covered. Trim tabs and horn balance on elevators (linked to flaps) and rudder. Rudder mass-balanced.

Undercarriage
Hydraulic retraction of all units. Vickers oleo-pneumatic shock-absorbers. MkI version had main wheels enclosed by doors—later Marks had larger wheels leaving tyre partially exposed. Vickers pneumatic wheel-brakes.

Powerplant
Two Bristol Pegasus, Pratt and Whitney Twin Wasp, or Bristol Hercules radial air-cooled or Rolls-Royce Merlin liquid-cooled engines. Three-bladed de Havilland, Rotol, Curtiss or Hamilton Standard propellers on air-cooled engines (except test installations) and three- or four-bladed Rotol on Merlin engines.

Standard fuel 634 imp gall in removable self-sealing wing tanks and 116 in nacelles—total 750 gall. In later Marks, long range tanks could be fitted in bomb-bay bringing total up to 1,305 gall giving nearly 17 hours endurance on ferry flights (about 2,000 miles).

Accommodation
Up to six crew, according to requirements. Could be flown solo.

Armament
MkI—three hydraulically operated Vickers turrets—nose, tail and ventral. Single Browning gun in nose, twin in tail, and single in retractable under turret. Nash and Thompson turret controls. Frazer-Nash ventral turret substituted for Vickers. Later had FN turrets, 2-gun front and 2- or 4-gun rear. Ventral deleted in favour of Vickers 'K' gas operated or Browning belt-fed .303in window-mounted beam guns. Warload—bombs (up to 18 250lb in 3 cells or one 4,000lb 'Cookie' in Type 423 bomb cell) or mines or two 18in torpedoes and/or long range tank(s) as required.

Dimensions
See Appendix 1.

Right. A cutaway drawing of the Wellington I by the late J. H. Clark of *The Aeroplane./Courtesy of Flight*

Below: The second production Wellington, L4213 seen at Eastleigh, Southampton, the home of Supermarine, in 1938. It has acquired the two aerial masts characteristic of early Mk Is and a D/F loop. The after mast was later removed./*Vickers*

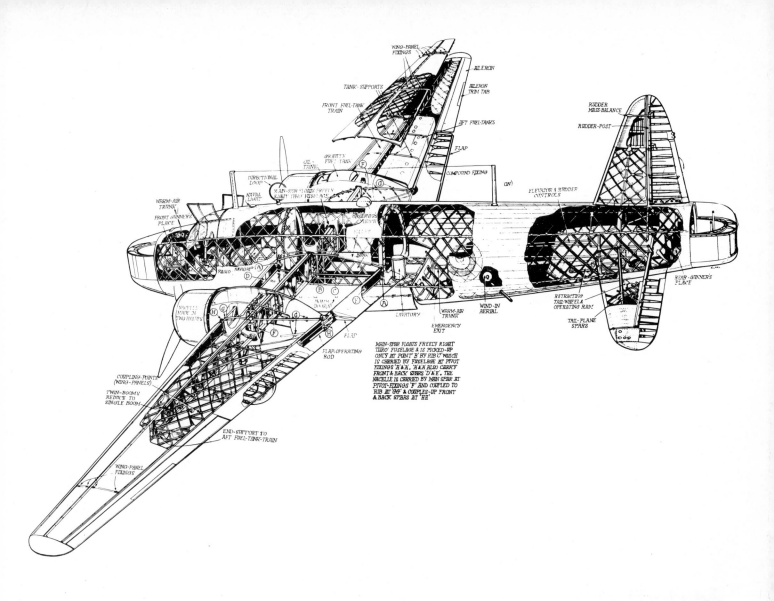

WING-PANEL FIXINGS

AILERON

AILERON TRIM TAB

TANK-SUPPORTS

AFT FUEL-TANKS

FRONT FUEL-TANK TRAIN

FLAP

RUDDER MASS-BALANCE

RUDDER-POST

COMPOUND FIXING

OIL-TANK

GRAVITY FUEL TANK

(ON)

DIRECTIONAL LOOP

ELEVATOR & RUDDER CONTROLS

NAVIG. LIGHT

MAIN-SPAR FLOATS FREELY ABOUT THRO' FUSELAGE

WARM-AIR TRUNK

OBSERVER'S SWITCH

FRONT GUNNER'S PLACE

FLIGHT

BUNK

RADIO

NAVIGATOR

RETRACTING TAIL-WHEEL & OPERATING RAM

REAR-GUNNER'S PLACE

NACELLE MADE IN TWO HALVES

LAVATORY

WARM-AIR TRUNK

WIND-IN AERIAL

TAIL-PLANE SPARS

EMERGENCY EXIT

FLAP

FLAP-OPERATING ROD

MAIN-SPAR FLOATS FREELY RIGHT THRO' FUSELAGE & IS PICKED-UP ONLY AT POINT 'B' BY RIB 'C' WHICH IS CARRIED BY FUSELAGE AT PIVOT FIXINGS 'A' & 'A'. 'A' & 'A' ALSO CARRY FRONT & BACK SPARS 'D' & 'E'. THE NACELLE IS CARRIED BY MAIN SPAR AT PIVOT-FIXINGS 'F' AND COUPLED TO RIB AT 'GG' & COUPLES-UP FRONT & BACK SPARS AT 'HH'

COUPLING-POINTS (WING-PANELS)

TWIN-BOOMS REDUCE TO SINGLE BOOM

END-SUPPORT TO AFT FUEL-TANK-TRAIN

WING-PANEL FIXINGS

Cockpit and Controls

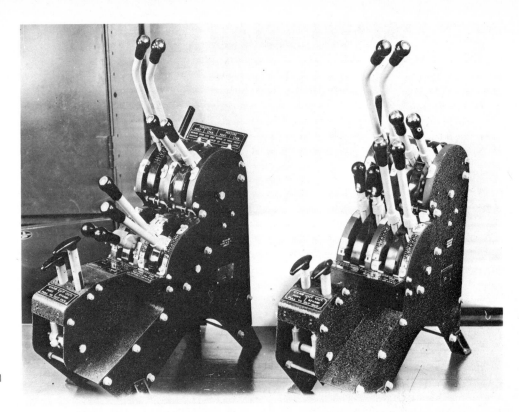

Left: The pilot's instrument panel of a Hercules engined Wellington. The electrical propeller control at upper right gives the clue./*Vickers*

Right: The throttle box of a Mk I Wellington showing the controls in the open and closed positions./*Vickers*

Below: Radio operator's position in a late model Wellington. The radio is a TR 1154/1155 (Transmitter/Receiver) set./*Vickers*

Type 271 B.9/32, K4049 first flew June 15, 1936, pilot J. Summers, at Brooklands. Crashed at Waldringfield 1½ miles east of Martlesham Heath, Suffolk, on the afternoon of Monday, April 19, 1937, pilot Maurice Hare. Engines 915hp Pegasus X. One built. First public appearance Hendon Air Pageant June 1936. Suggested name 'Crécy', changed to Wellington. Production of 180 ordered August 15, 1936.

Type 285 Spec 29/36. First production aircraft. MkI, L4212 first flew December 23, 1937, pilot J. Summers, at Brooklands. Engines Pegasus XX, changed to XVIII April 12, 1938, so becoming production *Type 290*. Delivered to Martlesham January 25, 1938. By end of 1938, 34 delivered. By outbreak of war, six squadrons in service in No 3 Group. By end September 1939, 210 delivered, the order book being 800. By March 12, 1940, 380 completed, 173 in squadrons and by April 14, 433 completed, 289 in squadrons. The last delivered to 38 Sq on August 8, 1939. Eighteen ordered by New Zealand—*Type 403*—delivered to 75 Sq, Vickers nose and tail turrets, FN ventral. L4215 first to a squadron (99, Mildenhall); L4221 bombing trials; L4244 for Royal Navy as transport and flying classroom for ASV training; L4255 converted to ambulance by ATA; L7770 first (of three) from Chester. Total built— Weybridge 178, Chester 3, Total 181. At least 11 converted to DWI MkII (Gipsy Six) standard at Croydon, including prototype L4212 and No 2 from Chester L7771. Cost of L4212 £82,150. Later aircraft about £14,900.

Left: The slender appearance from this angle of the B.9/32 belies the Wellington's ultimate shape and its true purpose as a bomber with, for those days, a formidable load and a high performance./*Vickers*

Above: The first of 11,460 production Wellingtons, L4212 is pushed over the River Wey onto Brooklands aerodrome./*Vickers*

Wellington L4212 taking off from Brooklands early in 1938. It first flew on December 23, 1937 powered by Pegasus XX engines. These were changed for the Pegasus XIII with two-speed superchargers the following April./ *Vickers*

The fourth Wellington, L4215 with mass-balanced elevators which were fitted temporarily. This aircraft was the first to be delivered to No 99 Squadron in October, 1938./ *Vickers*

The first Wellington to fly from Chester factory, Mk I, L7770 taking off on August 2, 1939. The difficulties of getting it out of the unfinished factory and off the waterlogged aerodrome were such that it had to be taken to Weybridge for testing./*Vickers*

Type 408 MkIA. Engines 1,050hp Pegasus XVIII. FN5 nose, FN10 tail and FN9 ventral turrets, each with two Browning machine guns. Eighteen delivered to 75 Sq as *Type 412.* First three delivered (N2865-7) just before outbreak of war, two to 149 Sq; MkIA based on MkII rather than MkI, interchangeable engine capability (not used), stressed for 28,000lb gross, strengthened undercarriage, larger wheels and chassis moved forward for CG purposes. Bomb gear and oxygen equipment as MkII, astrodome and fuel jettison pipes. (CMkIA modified as transport by RAF Hendon—became MkXV—converted at Gatwick and Brooklands). Extensively used for bombing and mine-laying. At least one (L7788 of 311 Sq) evaluated by Luftwaffe in German markings after forced landing in 1940. Four converted at Brooklands as DWI MkI (Ford)—P2516, 2511, 2518, 2521. Others (probably three) converted in Middle East—including one MkIC. MkIB (*Type 409*) proposed but not built. Total built: 187—Weybridge 170 (including DWI) and Chester 17.

The Central Gunnery School at Sutton Bridge, Yorks, operated most types of aircraft in the RAF. This formation comprises a Wellington IA, N2887, a Spitfire IIA and an early Allison-engined Mustang. The Wellington had an interesting history. It was one of those originally allocated to the RNZAF but not delivered, was built at Weybridge and was photographed in 1943 by Charles Brown while at CGS. It was subsequently converted into a C Mk XV by Vickers and used as a transport with its turrets removed. It is seen here fitted with a VHF whip aerial for communicating with the fighters./*Charles Brown*

Right: A Weybridge-built Wellington IA, N2912 wearing the code of 108 Squadron at the end of November, 1939. At this time, 108 Squadron was a training squadron in No 6 Group, at Bicester, Oxon. The fuselage bears traces of fabric repairs made necessary by ice being slung from the propeller blades./*Flight*

Below: New and repaired Wellingtons awaiting test at Weybridge. The aircraft at each end of the line bear squadron codes—that of NH-S being the pre-war code of 38 Squadron. The second from the left is a IA or IC, the first of which was not flown until just before the War so it is probably the first Mk IA, L7773, brought from Chester for examination. The crew are (L to R) Hugh Hemsley, Maurice Summers (brother of 'Mutt', pilot) and R. C. (Bob) Handasyde. The date, about the outbreak of war./*Vickers*

The Broughton Wellington
7th. Nov. 1940

Type 415 MkIC. By far the most widely used Pegasus-engined variant. MkXVIII engines (1,050hp). Incorporated most improvements up to MkII standard. Ventral turret deleted, FN turrets fore and aft (two guns each). Vickers 'K' or Browning guns in beam triangular windows—incorporated in all subsequent Marks. Improved hydraulics, 24 volt electrical system and DR compass. *Type 423* modified enabled 4,000lb bomb to be carried. First Blackpool-built aircraft—X3160. Torpedo-bomber prototype AD646 tested by Torpedo Development Unit (TDU) at Gosport and many subsequently delivered as torpedo aircraft. The MkIC, largely inspired by T. C. L. Westbrook and, for its power, proved an ideal compromise for numerous missions. Aircraft presented by public subscription to the RAF (at about £15,000 each) totalled at least 27 including 15 MkICs, one each III and X. The Broughton Wellington, R1333 was a IC subscribed by the contractors, sub-contractors and employees at the Chester (Broughton) Works. Unhappily, it crashed on delivery to No 99 Sq. A replacement of the same name, R1516, was delivered to 311 Sq and lost on operations. Total built: 2,685—Weybridge 1,052, Blackpool 50 and Chester 1,583.

Type 298 MkII (Prototype), *Type 406* (Production). Prototype L4250, 38th MkI airframe. First flew at Brooklands March 3, 1939. Variant powered by 1,145hp Merlin X as first of three designed in case of supply difficulties with Pegasus. Two turrets—FN5 (nose) and FN10 (tail). Design began January, 1938 as engine change modification and aircraft stayed at Boscombe Down for some months. Work on it ceased in October 1939, although modifications continued to be developed which were fed into IC production line. When finally put into production, MkII had a better performance than MkIC. Second prototype, R3221 was converted IC. First order for 200. Principal mods: 24 volt electrics, VSG pumps for 1,000lb/sq in aircraft services, 300lb turret hydraulics, cabin heating, astrodome. Rotol props. Tailplane area increased to counter instability. *Type 423* bomb beam for carrying 4,000lb bomb—first conversions W5389, 5399, 5400. This mod subsequently approved for IC, II and all later Marks and did not itself require separate mark of aircraft. First operational use—two dropped on Emden by MkIIs of 9 and 149 Squadrons on March 31/April 1, 1941. Other experimental MkIIs included: mods to prototype L4250 mounting large dorsal turret for Vickers 40mm self-loading gun with fully automatic predictor sight (*Type 416*). This resulted in control difficulties and original vertical tail was changed to twin, strut-braced fins on tailplane. Vickers 'S' 40mm gun also tested in nose of Z8416 (*Type 439*), complete with range-finder sight and predictor, intended for Vickers twin-engined high-altitude fighter (*Type 432*). Several examples of the Merlin-engined MkII were used as test beds for early jet engine experiments, at least one of which was seen on flights over East Anglia trailing black smoke. *Type 445* had a Rover W2B/23 jet mounted in the extreme tail (Z8570/G), converted to *Type 450* with a BTH W2B. *Type 470* had a BTH W2B—W5389/G. This aircraft had Merlin 62 engines and extended MkVI wings. *Type 486* mounted a W2/700 (W5518/G) and had Merlin 62s and MkVI wings, enabling it to reach 36,000ft Total built: 401—all at Weybridge.

The prototype Wellington II, L4250 was used for experiments with a 40 mm Vickers gun mounted in a large dorsal turret mounted in a stressed-skin section built specially for it. The gunner had an offset cupola and stability troubles resulting from this made it necessary to replace the standard fin by two smaller units which were, in effect, upper halves of normal fins./*IWM*

The prototype Wellington II, 38th airframe, was L4250. The engines were Rolls-Royce Merlin Xs. Numerous modifications were made to this aircraft at various times. It is seen here with the original exhausts and wooden 'Jablo' bladed Rotol propellers./*Vickers*

Left & Below: In addition to Mk II Z8570 (see colour plate), two other Mk IIs were converted for testing tail-mounted Whittle-type jets. Shown is W5389/G with Mk VI wings and engines and a W2B jet in the tail with 'ear' type intakes, Type 470./*Vickers*

Above & Right: The Power Jets W2/700 engine installed in the tail of Wellington II W5518/G, a hybrid aircraft with Mk VI wings and Merlin 60 engines. It reached 36,000 ft. It also created a stir when it crossed over Brooklands at low level with both propellers feathered after a shallow dive, making very little noise but it could not maintain level flight on the jet alone. The intakes were flush-mounted on the rear end of the fuselage of this Vickers Type 486./ *Vickers and IWM*

Type 299 MkIII (Prototype), *Type 417* (Production). First flew May 19, 1939, at Brooklands. Second variant, with 1,425hp Hercules III engines. Production aircraft with 1,590hp Hercules XI using 100 octane fuel. Prototype L4251, 39th MkI airframe. Turrets, two-gun FN5 (nose), two-gun FN4 (early aircraft) or four-gun FN20A (tail). Initial design began early 1938 using Hercules HEISM with two-stage superchargers and DH props. Engines at first unsatisfactory so a MkIC, P9238, was converted, using Hercules III and Rotol electric props. This was first powerplant installation and mods included de-icing, balloon cable cutters, windscreen wipers, Low-drag FN21A ventral turret proposed but eventually FN20A tail turret and beam guns adopted. First FN20A aircraft flew March 1940 (L4251). The MkIII became the main strike weapon of Bomber Command until replaced by the four-engined heavies. Entered squadron service with 9 Sq, June 22, 1941 at Honington. Cleared for glider-towing up to the weight of a Horsa (15,750lb) using a yoke bracket mounted aft of bomb bay. First MkIII converted X3268. Could also carry ten paratroops plus four 350lb equipment containers. Other MkIIIs modified included development of MkX and beyond (X3595); X3224 which spent much time at the RAE on engine cooling experiments, including propeller-mounted fans for tropical use; BK537 (*Type 451*) used by Rotol for airscrew tests; X3479 tested at Sherburn-in-Elmet in August 1942 for dropping MkIA Ordnance Smooth Bore Smith gun and parachute team; BJ895 which took part in the first experiments in the development of the Dambuster bombs, two being mounted in the open bomb bay and dropped off the Chesil Beach, Dorset. MkIIIs took part in the last Bomber Command Wellington operation, October 8, 1943. One of the best of the Wellingtons—it could be looped with ease. Total built: 1,519—Weybridge 2, Blackpool 780 and Chester 737.

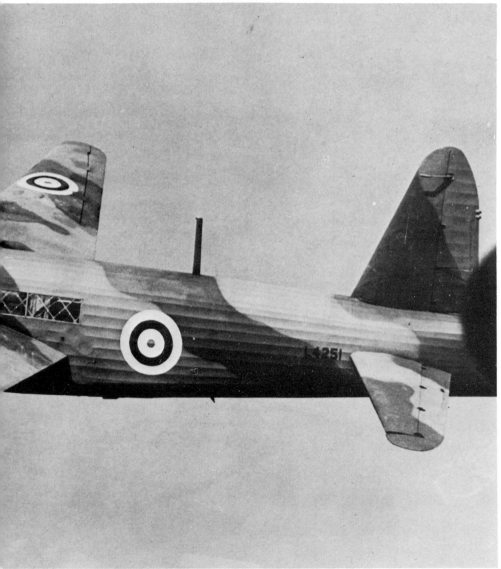

Above left: The original Hercules installation was not satisfactory and Mk IC. P9238 was converted on the Chester line to take Hercules IIIs and Rotol electric propellers. It is seen with a mock-up of the Frazer-Nash FN 20A tail turret for 4 guns. This became the production Mk III./*Vickers*

Above: Wellington IIIs and (in the distance) Xs of 30 OTU, Hixon, Staffs. The fuel bowser bears the markings B/93 indicating the Group./*IWM*

The prototype Mk III, L4251 was the 39th Mk I airframe. It was converted so as to use the Hercules HEISM as an alternative to the Pegasus. It is here seen with DH 'bracket' type propellers./*Vickers*

Right: Barnes Wallis's earliest experiments with the 'Dambusting' bouncing bomb were undertaken in Mk II BJ895 seen here with two dummy weapons in the bomb-bay. The bombs, which were spun before dropping, were tested between December 4 and 15, 1942, with 'Mutt' Summers flying and Wallis bomb-aiming. The aircraft flew from Warmwell, Dorset and dropped the weapons off the Chesil Beach./*Vickers*

Below: Air experience for Air Training Corps cadets was a regular commitment. A group are here boarding a Mk III for a training flight./ *BOP, IWM*

Type 410 MkIV (Prototype), *Type 424* (Production). First flew early December 1940 at Chester—R1220, pilot Maurice Hare. Third variant, based on IC and III experience, using 1,050hp Twin Wasp R-1830-S3C4-G ordered by France but not delivered. Turrets as MkIII. Engines obtained early in war as airframe production outstripped engines and Merlins were required for fighters. Excessive propeller noise from Hamilton Standard propellers—changed to cropped Curtiss electric units. Test pilot Tommy Lucke made power-off approach to Brooklands on delivery of prototype from Chester resulting in double engine failure at last minute from carburettor icing. Aircraft force landed at Addlestone, straddling River Wey. Several MkIVs sent to Boscombe for test and development including Z1248 up to 31,000lb gross for engine trials; Z1244 for Lindholme Air Sea Rescue equipment trials. First delivery June 2, 1941—Squadron deliveries (300, 301, 458 Sq) from August. First operation October 16, 1941. Total built: 220—all at Chester.

Below: The prototype Wellington Mk IV, R1220 emerging from the Flight Shed at Chester. The engines are Pratt and Whitney Twin Wasps. The Hamilton Standard propellers in this installation turned out to be excessively noisy and were later changed to Curtiss electric units./*Vickers*

Bottom: 'And we learnt about carburettor icing from that'. Mk IV prototype, at roll-out from Chester works; it suffered a double engine failure on the approach to Weybridge and ended up straddling the River Wey at Addlestone, Surrey./*Vickers*

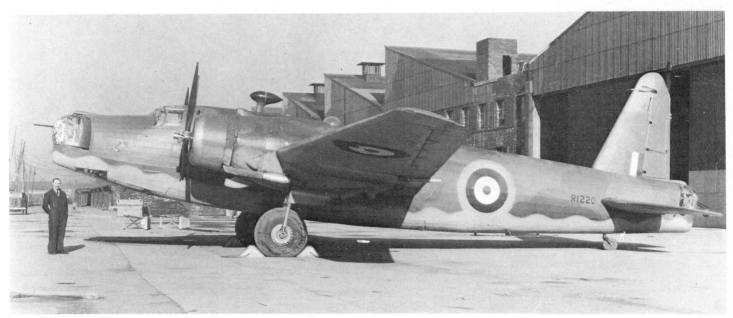

Type 407 MkV. Various Hercules installations (initially III), *Types 421, 426, 436.* First pressure-cabin, high altitude ('stratosphere bomber') development. Intended as a bomber at altitudes above ceiling of enemy fighters. Development delayed by DWI work, Vickers being asked to investigate possibilities in 1938 and Beaverbrook insisted on priority after Dunkirk evacuation at end of May 1940. First order for two prototypes May 1939—one with Hercules and one with Merlin (MkVI). Crew of three in a pressure-cabin giving ground level pressure up to 10,000ft (7lb/sq in internally, max). Bomb load 1,000lb, endurance 9.6hr. Engines to be turbo-supercharged Hercules VIII and XI but these did not come up to expectations so production concentrated on MkVI. Twelve had been ordered plus 120 MkVI (q.v.) Only three built. These provided the basis for pressure-cabins for Spitfire and Westland Welkin. Numerous problems encountered concerning freezing grease and oil due to intense cold at high altitude, as well as internal air-conditioning and heating difficulties, all of which were eventually overcome. Two prototypes R3298, 3299 built at Foxwarren, Cobham. Only one production aircraft built at VAX1 (Vickers Armstrong's Extension—One) Smiths Lawn, Windsor Great Park.

Above left: Partially completed Mk V–VI fuselage showing the front support of the pressure cabin./*Vickers*

Above: The first installation of a pressure cabin in a Wellington fuselage at Weybridge./*Vickers*

Left: The prototype Mk V, R3298. Assembly is almost complete./*Vickers*

Centre right: Crew compartment of a pressure cabin, seen from the rear door. The pilot's seat is mounted on the 'shelf' with the navigator/bomb aimer ahead of him. The radio operator sits behind him. The pilot's head projects into a pressurised dome, visibility ahead and downwards being minimal for landing although the dome is offset to port./*Vickers*

Below right: A Wellington pressure cabin showing the rear entry door./*Vickers*

Type 431 MkVI. Type 442(Production VIA, Vs converted), *Type 449* (VIG). Developed in parallel with MkV using 1,600hp Merlin 60 series engines. Designed for high altitude bombing using the then secret Norden bomb sight. Single FN70 pressurised rear turret was planned but this was replaced by remotely operated FN20A, locked at altitude. Prototype W5795 (built at Foxwarren) reached 40,000ft. At one stage had 12ft extra span, later removed. It subsequently crashed. Crew: pilot, navigator, wireless operator, and bomb-aimer. Cabin pressure 7.5lb/sq in, proof tested to 15lb/sq in. Length 18ft 3in, diameter 5ft 5in, 3ft 2in entry door at rear. Pilot's view through plastic dome, kept clear by warm air. Air from engine-driven compressors drawn from inside fuselage. Temperatures down to -71°C caused serious lubrication and air-conditioning difficulties—eventually overcome. By the time MkVI reached operational status, the Mosquito had far surpassed it in speed, carrying similar 4,000lb bomb load at almost as great altitudes but without the need of a pressure-cabin. Orders: Total 132—included one prototype each of MkV and VI and 130 production. Three MkVs completed (two prototypes and one production), nine cancelled. Only 64 MkVIs completed, including 18 re-engined MkVs. Assembled and flown at VAX1. W5795 and W5800 had 6ft wing extensions for high altitude experiments. W5801 and W5802 were attached to No 109 Sq for special radio experiments at Stradishall in March 1942. W5802 then went to RAE in May. W5801 stayed on at Stradishall till July 1942 and is reported to have undertaken at least two operations over enemy territory in daylight. Thirty-two of the production MkVIs were intended for experiments with 'Oboe' blind bombing radio aid—of which three (DR481-3) were trainers. Two MkVIs had *Type 423* (4,000lb) bomb gear (DR480 and 484).

Below: A very rare picture showing three production Wellington VIs in the Bellman hangar at Smith's Lawn, Windsor Great Park where they were assembled. /*Vickers*

Far left: The starboard Merlin 60 of a Mk VI. The main radiator is flanked by oil and intercooler radiators./*Vickers*

Above left: One of the Mk VIA Wellingtons showing the original Mk V nose and Merlin engine./*Vickers*

Above: Wellington VI, DR484 at Brooklands. Picture shows the production-type nose. This was the second of two fitted with Type 423 bomb gear for carrying 4,000 lb bombs. No tail turret is fitted. Note 'Lancaster' type cowlings./*IWM*

Left: Wellington Mk VIA, W5798, the first of a batch of 27 originally built as Mk Vs and re-engined with Merlins. This aircraft was one of two used for experiments at the RAE and at Boscombe Down with the Sperry gyro bomb sight./*IWM*

Type 430 MkVII. An improved Merlin XX engined MkII. 150 ordered in May 1941—later cancelled. Prototype (T2545) flew from Weybridge and became test-bed for Merlin 60 series engine at Hucknall.

Types 428, 429 MkVIII. A Coastal Command (General Reconnaissance) version of MkIC with 1,050hp Pegasus XVIII engines. Built in day and night versions and equipped with ASV MkII ('Stickleback') radar. Day version equipped for torpedo-dropping and night variant had Leigh-light. The under turret position was used for retractable Leigh-light. Front and rear FN7A turrets in torpedo aircraft. Very important in the Battle of the Atlantic, this was first combination using radar (ASV) down to a distance where 'clutter' obscured the echo and then visual contact using Leigh searchlight. Originally called 'DWI MkIII', the light was proposed using the generator of the first DWI magnetic ring and a naval searchlight. Was in competition with an alternative nose-mounted wide-angle Helmore light which used storage batteries. Leigh-light eventually used trickle-charged storage batteries and ventral mounting, combining the best of both. No nose-turret in night version—front position occupied by light operator. Helmore light conversion T2977. First Leigh-light aircraft ES986. First use of light in MkVIII on June 3, 1942. Total built (all at Weybridge) 394—Bombers 65, Torpedo-bombers 271 and Leigh-light version 58.

Left: The first Coastal Command Wellington was the Mk VIII. This one, W5674 DF-D is one of the second Weybridge-built batch and is believed to have been flown by 331 Squadron before going overseas. It is equipped for daylight shipping strikes, having a front turret and no Leigh-light. The 'Stickleback' antennae are associated with ASV Mk II./*IWM*

Below left: This Wellington VIII, HX419 is a Leigh-light version for night operations. The retracted light is aft of the open bomb doors and the front gunner's position is occupied in flight by the light operator. ASV Mk II is fitted. Built at Weybridge, mid 1942.

Below: Mk VIII, HF857 has run into a small crater on Malta's Luqa aerodrome. This is the daylight version with ASV Mk II and the starboard wing 'Yagi' aerial is shown to advantage./*IWM*

Type 437 MkIX. Special troop-carrying version of the MkIA—only one built, P2522.

Type 440 MkX (Prototype), *Type 448* (Production). Developed from, and similar in appearance to MkIII but with later 1,675hp Hercules VI or XVI (with auto-carburettor and single lever control) engines. External difference was long carburettor intake. Internally, structure strengthened for higher gross weight by use of newly-developed light-alloys equivalent in strength to mild steel. Nearly half as many again built as MkIC. First flew at Blackpool—X3374 and X3595 (MkIIIs converted). First production aircraft—DF609· Blackpool) and HE147 (Chester). The MkX had the best performance of all Wellingtons and was built in the largest numbers. After four-engined heavy bombers replaced the Wellington in Bomber Command, the MkX remained, with decreasing number of ICs and IIIs on general duties. Above all, it fulfilled every crew training role in Bomber and Coastal Commands. It remained as an important strategic bomber in the Middle East, Sicily and Italy until the end of the war in Europe and then in the Far East until VJ Day. The last Wellingtons, T10s, to serve in the RAF remained in training units, until finally withdrawn from Nos 1 and 6 ANS in March 1953, to be replaced by Valettas. The last left with 1 ANS was LP806. Other MkXs included HF616 and 621 were used for high altitude tests of the Hercules 38 with single GEC turbo-blowers; LN715 became *Type 602*, testing the Dart turboprop; LN718 mounted Hercules 100s for the Halifax and Viking installations, NA857 was intended for the Napier Naiad turboprop but was not converted; RP484 was involved in noise tests at Bristol—including both props feathered. RP468 became G-ALUH and was equipped with experimental tail radar; RP590 was the last Wellington to be delivered (from Blackpool); MF648 is the last surviving example in the RAF Museum, Hendon. At least six MkXs were sold as trainers to France. Total built: 3,803—Blackpool 1,369 and Chester 2,434.

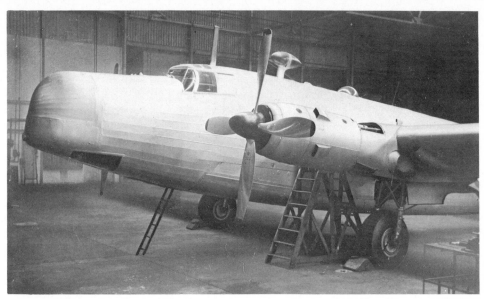

Above: One of several Mk Xs converted as flying test beds. This is LN718 fitted with Viking-type engines and propellers and a water spray for testing the electrical de-icing system. The location, Staverton, Cheltenham.

Above right: Two views of LN175, a turretless Mk X modified for flight-testing the Rolls-Royce Dart turbo-prop developed for the Viscount and many later aircraft. This aircraft, like other late model Mk Xs had aerodynamic as well as mass balances on the rudder./*Flight, Vickers*

Left: This Mk X was built at Blackpool as a Mk III and served with No 75 (NZ) Squadron. This and X3374 were converted to Mk X standard as prototypes. Seen here at Brooklands, X3595 has Hydromatic propellers and the beam gun position is clearly visible./*IWM*

Right: A Hercules engine is swung into position for mounting on a Mk X at Chester. The diagonal fabric covering and 'trainer' nose can be seen./*Vickers*

Type 454 GR MkXI (with ASV MkII), *Type 458* (ASV MkIII Prototype), *Type 459* (ASV MkIII Production). This was the Coastal Command torpedo-bomber—daylight version of the MkX based on experience gained from the MkVIII torpedo version. Engines were Hercules VI or XVI. ASV MkII or III (centimetric) radar. Total built: 180—Weybridge 105 and Blackpool 75. At least one was sold to France.

Type 455 GR MkXII. Anti-submarine Leigh-light equipped variant of MkXI. Chin-mounted ASV MkIII radar. Hercules VI or XVI engines. Leigh-light mounted in ventral position. Total built: 58—Weybridge 50 and Chester 8.

Type 466 GR MkXIII, 490 (Blackpool developed conversion of MkXI) developed from XI with Hercules XVII engines developing 1,735hp at low level. ASV MkII daylight torpedo-bomber. At least eight sold to Greece. Total built: 844—Weybridge 42 and Blackpool 802.

Right: One of several Wellingtons used by the Royal Navy, HZ361 is a Mk XI. The location of the ASV Mk II side aerials on the fuselage can still be seen./*FAA Museum*

Below: The first Wellington to be fitted with centimetric ASV Mk III radar in service was the Mk XII. The aircraft shown is MP684 fitted with a Leigh-light. The beam gun casting a shadow down the fuselage is a Browning ·303 in MG./*Vickers*

Centre right: Blackpool-built Mk XIII, JA412 equipped with ASV Mk II radar. It is flying among the Greek islands carrying relief supplies to isolated communities at the end of the war in Europe and possibly belonged to No 221 Squadron. Note the upper beam gun position above the flare chute./*IWM*

Below right: A number of Wellingtons were sold to France for reconnaissance use by the Aéronavale. This example, MP771 is a Mk XIII, a daylight torpedo-bomber with low-altitude Hercules XVII engines. The aerials on the side of the fuselage are sideways-looking radar, part of the ASV Mk II installation./*ECDA*

Type 467 GR MkXIV, developed from MkXII—Leigh-light and ASV MkIII centimetric radar. Hercules XVII engines. Many sold to France. Total built: 841—Weybridge 53, Blackpool 250 and Chester 538. *CMkXV*, was CMkIA converted for transport duties by Vickers and further developed by the RAF. No turrets but some had painted turrets as camouflage. *CMkXVI* was CMkIC converted for transport duties by Vickers and further developed by the RAF.

Type 487 TMkXVII, Service conversion of MkXI for night fighter crew training. Mosquito-type nose with SCR720 AI radar.

Right: A nearly-completed Mk XIV jacked up for an undercarriage retraction test at Chester works. The flexible mounting for two Browning machine guns in the nose are visible. These were used as 'persuaders' against U-Boat crews who attempted to fight it out on the surface. There was no front power-operated turret on Leigh-light aircraft./*Vickers*

Below: One of the first batch of Wellington XIVs built at Chester, HF167 is flying with its Leigh-light lowered, a rare sight by day. This aircraft has ASV Mk III and also a radio altimeter.

Above right: Wellington XIVs operating from St Eval, Cornwall, belonging to No 304 (Polish) Squadron. Following the Allied landings in Normandy on June 6, 1944, large numbers of U-Boats attempted to interfere with the heavy cross-channel traffic and those without the new 'schnorkel' breathing tube were attacked repeatedly while surfaced by Coastal Command. One of seven sunk in the 12 days following the invasion was U 441 (Hartmann), a commerce raider sunk by a Wellington of this squadron and flown by Flt Lt Antoniewicz who straddled the boat with six 250 lb depth charges. /IWM

Right: Wellington XIVs of 458 RAAF Squadron at Gibraltar in 1944. The original print shows four Martinets, a Swordfish and a Beaufighter in the background. /IWM

What's in a Name

The Wellington's name was a natural follow-on to that of its predecessor, the Wellesley. All British military aircraft prior to, and most of them during, World War 2 were codified according to purpose (B); sequence of number (9); and the year of specification issue (32)—hence the number of the Wellington specification—B9/32. The competition for the 'twin-engined medium day bomber' contract to this specification was issued on October 20, 1932. Designs were submitted by Vickers, Handley Page and Bristol and those chosen were the Vickers *Type 271* and the Handley Page Hampden.

Apart from its type number, the new Vickers project at first lacked a name. It had been customary for military aircraft to be given a name of an appropriate town associated with the area where it was built, or of an animal, usually of an aggressive nature, and an alliteration with the maker's name was the normal practice. The original name 'Crécy' never became established and 'Wellington' was eventually adopted. Various explanations were given for this change but the most logical was to adopt that of the great British soldier whose family name Wellesley had been used for the aeroplane's predecessor from Weybridge. Apart from perpetuating the memory of the Duke of Wellington (1769-1852)—whose famed reputation as a rigid disciplinarian caused him to be known as the 'Iron Duke'—it had a fairly slender connection with an aeroplane whose flexibility, indeed elasticity in flight was a byword! Nevertheless, it continued the established practice of using the initial letter 'W' for aircraft incorporating geodetic structures designed by Barnes Wallis.

Nomenclature is a subject which invites puns. The Wellington was responsible for its fair share of these. The rotund, 'well-fed' appearance of the Wellington was soon to be compared with that of Popeye's stout Hamburger-devouring friend in the famous strip-cartoon in the London *Daily Mirror* newspaper. His name was 'J. Wellington Wimpy' and so the bomber widely became known as the 'Wimpy', a name by which it will always be remembered. It was no coincidence, either, that the great German port of Hamburg was suffering more than a little from the Vickers bomber at that time. This was a particularly apt double pun, born of the irreverent atmosphere of the crew-room in the stress of the war. The name is still preserved today by the well-known nation-wide chain of 'Wimpy' hamburger bars operated by J. Lyons & Co. Such is the fame of the name Wellington that it still holds an important place in the daily lives of many of us—an impression of the Iron Duke and a battle scene appears on the back of the present five pound note. The Wellington has also given its name to at least one pub—the best known in Hastings, Sussex.

The Popeye cartoon from the *Daily Mirror* of September 6, 1943. Popeye's hamburger-eating friend, J. Wellington Wimpy lent his name to the famous bomber.

'Directional Wireless Installation'
or 'Down With 'Itler'

One of the most bizarre aircraft to be seen during World War II was the DWI Wellington. At the end of 1939, G. R. Edwards, who was Manager of the Experimental Department at Weybridge, was personally responsible in the production of a specially modified Wellington for exploding magnetic mines. Some years later, as Sir George Edwards, Chairman of British Aircraft Corporation, he recalled with nostalgia how the whole device was thought up, tested and put into operational service inside three months. This Wellington had a 51ft diameter ring containing an aluminium electro-magnetic coil suspended underneath for countering the menace of the first German 'Secret Weapon' of which Hitler had boasted, the magnetic sea mine. This new form of anti-shipping weapon which was dropped in numbers by low-flying German bombers, became a serious menace in coastal waters towards the end of 1939.

The system which operated with the DWI project required that every night, a set of photographs showing the progress made on the experimental aircraft during the day were sent to the First Lord of the Admiralty in order that he could see just how much had been done in 24 hours. The First Lord at that time was Winston Churchill. Under that sort of pressure, it is not surprising that the job was done in three months. In fact, Christmas 1939 was the time of peak effort, getting the aircraft ready for its first flight. The Experimental Department achieved a remarkable success in producing both an effective counter-measure to the highly dangerous mine without undue risk to the aircraft and, not least, an aircraft whose aerodynamics depended on highly theoretical calculations but which turned out to be perfectly satisfactory.

The finding, recovery and testing of the first magnetic mine, the devising of an effective means of destroying it safely, or of neutralising it, is a story in itself. The first was recovered intact due to gallant work by Naval specialists and the examination of its mechanism and the devising of an antidote were undertaken by the RAE at Farnborough and the Electro-Magnetics Group of the Admiralty Research Laboratory. Two methods were devised by the Admiralty—the electro-magnetic ring mounted on an aircraft for detonating the mines and the degaussing system for ships for neutralising them. Both were put in hand with all speed.

The aircraft ring was to be designed and made at Weybridge. Space was cleared in the main erecting shop for assembling the ring casing. Cranes were available and, by November 20, 1939 a start had been made on a turntable for making the coil. This was made of aluminium strip which was available in almost indefinite lengths, some two inches wide. It was wound into the coil on the turntable like a clock spring, with paper insulation wound with it. A balsa-wood fairing bound with tape provided a casing to reduce drag. The location of the ring on the Wellington was decided as the result of wind tunnel tests. In view of

Designed, built and tested in under three months was the first of four Mk IA Wellingtons converted at Weybridge while still on the factory line to DWI Mk I (Ford V-8). These three pictures were slightly retouched by the wartime censor to disguise the Brooklands background but nothing could hide the huge, 51 ft diameter ring for exploding German magnetic mines. The first flew just after Christmas, 1939, the Experimental Department having worked throughout the holiday. A further eleven Mk Is were subsequently converted by Rollason's at Croydon using a Gipsy Six in place of the Ford car engine to drive a more powerful generator and magnetising a 48 ft diameter ring.

the possibility of aerodynamic troubles, arrangements were made in November for the ring casing to be made in sections for transporting and, at first, it was proposed that they should be sent to Chester for assembly and testing. The first flight was to be made with the casing empty to test the aerodynamics and then flown back to Weybridge for the coil to be mounted in it. It was considered unsafe to make the first flight from Brooklands. The first Wellington to be modified was a MkIA straight off the Weybridge production line—P2516. Air Marshal Sir Wilfrid Freeman, Air Member for Development and Production, would only agree to the diversion of one MkIA from the urgently needed production and would have preferred that the small number of Armstrong Whitworth Ensigns available, transferred from BOAC's Empire routes to RAF communications duties, be used instead.

The Wellington installation was such that the magnetic field generated in the ring could be 'focussed' to some extent forward or aft of the midships line by adjusting the angle relative to the fore and aft datum of the aircraft. The detonation of a mine would be caused at, or immediately following, the peak effect of the magnetic field, and the incidental effect, if any, upon the aircraft then depended upon:

(a) Height—which must be low enough to ensure activation of the mine mechanism but not so low as to detonate the mine in the path of the aircraft.
(b) Speed—not so fast that the magnetic field peaked for too short a period for the mechanism to operate, yet fast enough in relation to aircraft height for the detonation and splash to miss the tail.
(c) The angle of incidence of the ring—with the aircraft in level flight—the ring would contribute a significant amount of lift and the consequent trim of the aircraft/ring combination needed very careful attention to ensure both level flight and the correct location of the magnetic field to give the desired effects.

The coil itself was energised by means of a Ford V-8 engine driving a 35kw (310amp) Maudeslay generator but Pierson considered that a more satisfactory solution would be to use a Gipsy Six aero-engine driving a 95kw generator. There was no problem in cooling the coil—air circulated within the casing from an intake at the front and outlets at sides and rear.

In view of Sir Wilfrid Freeman's wish that no more than one Wellington MkIA should be used, Handley Page Ltd was approached about using Harrows instead. There were about 60 redundant Harrows available and, for a short time, it was uncertain whether Harrows or Ensigns would in fact, be used. On December 13, however, Air Marshals Tedder and Sholto Douglas visited Weybridge for lunch and agreed that three MkIAs should be converted but asked for the job to be turned over to another firm for subsequent work. This suited Vickers as the DWI work was delaying another important project. It was then agreed that three conversions from the MkIA should be made 'off the production line' and that subsequent conversions would be made by Rollasons at Croydon, the

ring being made there as well, by the English Electric Co.

By Tuesday, December 19, the first coil was finished at Weybridge. The casing had been proof loaded the previous Sunday and sent to Boscombe Down the same day—a much more convenient arrangement than sending it to Chester as had been proposed previously. The selected aircraft (P2516) was test-flown and, after a frustrating delay of two days through bad weather, was flown to Boscombe Down to have the casing fitted.

A meeting was held at Farnborough on December 20, at which it was proposed that Handley Page should make the ring cases for future conversions for fitting by Rollasons. Most important, some very early Wellington Is were available and it was decided to try out a Gipsy Six/95kw generator combination in one of these, with a slightly smaller and lighter ring which while it gave a 50 per cent greater magnetic field saved 1,000lb installed weight.

On the following day, Thursday, P2516 having flown light to Boscombe, was fitted with its ring casing, test flown for handling by Mutt Summers and pronounced satisfactory. He immediately flew it back to Weybridge, for the ring to be attached to the casing. The whole assembly was being handled very carefully despite the high pressure for results. No undue risks were to be taken and Summers and Wallis were anxious that the wind at Brooklands should be in the best direction before flying off the second stage of the assembly. On December 27, 1939, the Wellington took off from Brooklands and returned to Boscombe for the Ford engine/generator set to be fitted. The Experimental Department at Weybridge under G. R. Edwards had worked with hardly a break for three months and throughout Christmas. The delivery flight to Boscombe was made by Summers flying solo. The aircraft '. . . had taken off excellently' to quote a contemporary memorandum from Alexander Dunbar, general manager of the Vickers aircraft companies to the chairman Sir Charles Craven, 'What wind there was, being in the right direction'. Squadron Leader Purvis, who

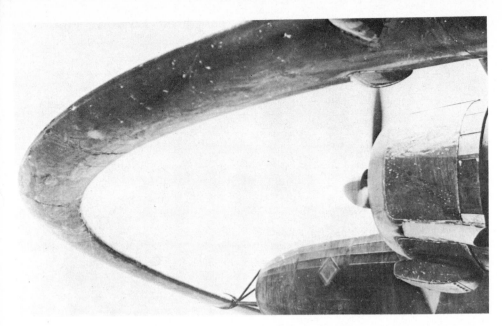

Several Wellingtons are believed to have been converted to the DWI Mk II configuration in the Middle East using parts sent from England. These included the only Mk IC conversions of which HX682 shown here is one example. It was based in the Canal Zone and operated by No 162 Squadron which officially undertook special radio and bomber support tasks in North Africa, particularly in coastal areas. Although the Royal Navy undertook the main bulk of mine-sweeping along the North African coast, No 162 Squadron was kept busy as well. In home waters, the Navy had equipped most ships with degaussing equipment some two years earlier./ *Vickers, IWM*

was to operate the aircraft, followed in Vickers own Miles Falcon communication aircraft.

The installation was completed on the night of December 28 but, once again, bad weather held up tests. There was snow on the bleak, exposed aerodrome on Salisbury Plain, making it too dangerous for full load trials to proceed next day. On the 30th, however, P2516 flew successfully in the hands of Summers. The Ford engine was not sufficiently cooled, however. R. C. Handasyde, then a flight test observer (soon to become a Vickers test pilot), vividly describes what it was like working in the stiflingly hot atmosphere of the Wellington's fuselage during the initial tests. He says 'I was in charge of the works at the back, which consisted of the Ford V-8 engine driving the dynamo to provide the current. We experimented with the first mine ever discovered by the Naval boys off the Medway. It was sticking up in the mud when the tide went out and they defused it—using rubber spanners or something. They took the magnetic part out and sent it down to Boscombe. There they stuck it out in the middle of the aerodrome. The DWI pilot was Bruin Purvis and we flew for about two hours, flying directly over the thing at 10ft, 20ft, 30ft, etc., then so many yards either side of it. Every time we flew past it, the magnetic thing clicked. The experts at Boscombe were able to get a beautiful polar diagram until we were too far out for it to dip. At that particular time at Boscombe, January, 1940, it was the coldest they had had for many years, something like -20 degrees C. Inside the Wimpy, the temperature was about 120 degrees F. I had to work stripped to the waist, sweating hard; it was most uncomfortable putting on an Irvin jacket afterwards. When they took the first one down to Manston for proper trials, they actually blew up a mine on their first sortie. They kept very low and it was pretty exciting sitting down at the back end of the Wimpy seeing the water suddenly heave up'.

Maurice Hare was one of the Weybridge test pilots during the time of the DWI development, prior to taking up the job of testing Wellingtons at the new Chester factory. 'It was very normal to fly' he said. 'I felt rather apprehensive at the sight of that awful great thing surrounding the cockpit. It was enormous. Otherwise, apart from being limited in speed, it handled perfectly normally but it was a weird feeling with this thing from (it seemed) wing-tip to wing-tip and well out beyond the nose. I well recall the rush to get it ready, a really intensive effort to get it out in time over Christmas, 1939. I also remember completely wrecking my very valuable wrist watch by being too near the thing when it was switched on in the Works. The magnetism completely wrecked the watch'.

Trevor Westbrook, the works manager, found that cooling could be improved by using air ducts. On December 30, RAE at Farnborough advised Vickers that four MkIAs instead of three, were to be converted at Weybridge, and that Tedder had agreed. It was also decided that old MkIs were to be used for the conversions which would be assembled at Croydon by Rollasons, using locally made English Electric coils, employing their own rig, to prevent needless delays. There would be no further interference with Vickers experimental work which was becoming more and more urgent.

Monday, January 8, 1940 was the day when word was passed from Boscombe to the Vickers board—'Summers says it works'.

Although design work for subsequent conversions with smaller rings was a Vickers responsibility, that was almost complete by this date. Farnborough would undertake the major modifications to the Wellington Is before flying them to Croydon for assembly of the ring and powerplant. Vickers kept their own assembly rig until all four MkIAs had been completed. These were to be known as DWI MkIs (Vickers *Type 418*) and the higher powered, smaller ring installations DWI MkII (Vickers *Type 419*).

A Wellington of 162 Squadron over Tripoli harbour soon after the Allies captured the town on January 23, 1943./*IWM*

By January 15, Weybridge's No 2 was ready to fly from Boscombe Down to Manston for trials in earnest over the Thames Estuary. A week later, No 3 had passed flight test and the coil was being tested before fitting to the casing. It was delivered to Boscombe on January 25 and completed two days later. The fourth followed soon after. Thursday, February 22 was a big day for all who had been involved in this hectic programme. Three DWI Wellingtons were flying that day and two mines were exploded quite safely. The thing worked indeed.

By the beginning of March, the DWI had become a routine matter for Vickers. On the 2nd, Summers flew over to Croydon and flight tested the first of the Wellington MkIs which had been modified by Rollasons.

Another ten were to be modified in England to DWI MkII standard, one of which was flown to the Middle East where several others were similarly converted. There, they performed equally valuable work clearing magnetic mines from the Suez Canal and North African harbours. They performed their work in effective, if ungainly fashion. They flew satisfactorily and the Experimental Department at Weybridge had the perhaps doubtful satisfaction of seeing photographs not only of their own 'baby' at work but also of a German version doing similar work clearing Allied mines. Before long, with the availability of suitable degaussing coils for ships, the DWI was superceded in British coastal waters although it continued for a time its work in the Middle East. The installation of the engine/generator set however gave rise to a development which was to revolutionise submarine warfare. This was called DWI MkIII but the title was a disguise, since it was for quite a different purpose—the Leigh-light.

RIP

From the issue of the original Air Ministry specification B.9/32 in October 1932 to the withdrawal of the last T.10 trainer in March 1953, the Wellington story covers more than two decades. And the story has not, in fact, ended yet since, happily, there is still just one example of the Wellington in existence. This is to be found in the Royal Air Force Museum at Hendon, about fifteen minute's walk from Colindale Underground station. The last example of the famous line—MF628 a TMk10—is now beautifully restored and is prominently displayed only yards from where the original Wellington prototype, the B.9/32 was first shown to the public in the RAF Display in 1936.

Long may it remind us of the same classic shape and reputation of a great British achievement that did so much to win a war whereby, through strength, mankind may hopefully live in comparative peace.

The sole surviving Wellington, MF628 in three
settings. As an RAF trainer, finished silver
and yellow, the T Mk 10 was built as a B Mk X,
converted after the war. Then, after its service
ended, MF628 returned to Vickers and is seen
at the RAeS Garden Party at Wisley in 1957.
By then, it had joined the Nash Collection of
Historic Aircraft and, finally, with the other items
of the Collection, it joined the RAF Museum
where it stands in a splendid setting at
Hendon./MOD, Vickers & Flight

Appendix 1 Wellington Data

Mark	Engines (2)	Duties	Weight loaded (lb)	Max speed at operational height (mph)	Normal range (miles)	Max range (miles)	Ceiling (feet)	Bomb load (lb)
I	Pegasus XVIII 1,050hp	Medium Bomber	24,850	245		2,200	21,600	4,500
IC	Pegasus XVIII 1,050hp	Medium Bomber	28,500	235	1,805	2,550	18,000	4,500
II	Merlin X 1,145hp	Medium Bomber	33,000	254	1,570	2,220	23,500	4,000
III	Hercules III or XI 1,425hp	Medium Bomber	34,500	255	1,470	2,085	22,000	4,500
IV	Twin-Wasp R-1830-S304-G 1,050hp	Medium Bomber	31,600	299	1,510	2,150	21,250	4,500
V	Hercules VIII approx. 1,600hp	High-Altitude Bomber	32,000	252	1,560	2,250	36,800	4,500
VI	Merlin 60 or 62 1,600hp	High-Altitude Bomber	30,450	300	1,510	2,180	38,500 40,000 with ext. wings	4,500
VIII	Pegasus XVIII 1,050hp	GR and Torpedo Bomber	30,000	235	1,805	2,550	19,000	4,500
X	Hercules VI or XVI 1,675hp	Medium Bomber	36,500	255	1,470	2,085	22,000	4,000
XI	Hercules VI or XVI 1,675hp	GR and Torpedo Bomber	36,500	256	1,400	2,020	19,000	4,500
XII	Hercules VI or XVI 1,675hp	Coastal Rec. Bomber	36,500	256	1,435	1,810	18,500	5,100
XIII	Hercules XVII 1,735hp	GR Bomber	36,500	250	1,390	1,700	16,000	5,000
XIV	Hercules XVII 1,735hp	GR Bomber	36,500	250	1,390	1,760	16,000	5,000
XVIII	Hercules XVII 1,735hp	Crew Trainer	36,500	255	1,470	2,065	22,000	—

Standard Version: Span 86ft 2in; length 64ft 7in; height 17ft 5in; wing area 640sq feet; crew either 5 or 6 (3 only in Marks 5 and 6).

Appendix 2

Works	(P)	I	IA	IA (DWI)	IC	IC (TB)	II	III	IV	V	VI	VIII	VIII (TB)	VIII (Leigh)	X	XI	XII	XIII	XIV	XVIII	Total
Weybridge	1	178	166	4	914	138	401	2	—	3	64	65	271	58	—	105	50	42	53	—	2,515
Blackpool	—	—	—	—	50	—	—	780	—	—	—	—	—	—	1,369	75	—	802	250	80	3,406
Chester	—	3	17	—	1,583	—	—	737	220	—	—	—	—	—	2,434	—	8	—	538	—	5,540
Total	1	181	183	4	2,547 (2,685)	138	401	1,519	220	3	64	65	271	58	3,803	180	58	844	841	80	11,461

DWI—Fitted with Magnetic Aluminium Ring. TB—Torpedo Bomber. Leigh—Equipped with Leigh Light. (P)—Prototype.

Note: These figures are 'as built', large numbers having been converted from one mark to another by order of the Ministry of Aircraft Production, while still on the production line.

Appendix 3   Wellington V and VI Production Details

Mark	Type	Engines	Canopy	Serials	No built	Remarks
V	421	Hercules III	Elliptical	R3298	1	First prototype MkV. Built at Foxwarren.
V	436	Hercules XI turbo-blowers	Elliptical	R3298		First prototype MkV. Built at Foxwarren.
V	407	Hercules VIII	Circular	R3299	1	Second prototype MkV. Built at Foxwarren.
V	426	Hercules VIII	Circular	W5796	1	First production MkV. Built at VAX1.
VI	431	Merlin 60	Circular	W5795	1	Prototype MkVI. Built at Foxwarren. Had 6ft wing extensions, later removed. Crashed.
VIA	442	Merlin 60	Circular	W5797	1	Became Rolls-Royce flying test bed. Not fully equipped. Built at VAX1.
VIA	442	Merlin 60	Circular	W5798-5815 DR471-479	27	Production aircraft, MkVs converted to Merlins. W5800 had extended wings, later removed. W5798, 5802 Sperry bomb sight trials at RAE and Boscombe. W5801, 5802 with 109 Squadron.
VI	431	Merlin 60	Elliptical	DR480,484	2	Production aircraft with *Type 423* (4,000lb) bomb gear.
VIG	449	Merlin 60	Elliptical	DR481-483/G	3	Trainers for special radio equipment ('Oboe').
VIG	449	Merlin 60	Elliptical	DR485-504/G DR519-527/G	29	Production aircraft, special radio equipment ('Oboe').
VI	431	Merlin 60	Elliptical	DR528/G	1	Production aircraft.

Total built 67; MkVs cancelled 9; MkVIs cancelled 56; total ordered 132.
Note:
MkVIA was Vickers' Ref. to MkV airframes re-engined with Merlin engines and finished to MkVI standard.

Chester-built Wellington IC, R1448 of 218 (Gold Coast) Squadron, the picture taken in mid 1941 when the Squadron was based at Marham, one of the 3 Group stations in Norfolk. It had the code HA-L when, on February 12, 1942 it flew 218's last Wellington operation, the Squadron having converted to Sterlings./*IWM*

The very last Wellington, Mk X, RP590 flies a farewell salute to the Blackpool factory where it was built. This, the last of the 11,460 production Wellingtons, was handed over to the RAF on October 25, 1945. This aircraft had a horn balanced rudder./*Charles Brown*